COLOUR COMBINATIONS

Vibrant interiors,
bold palettes

Marlous Snijder

Lannoo

TABLE OF CONTENTS

On choosing colour	06
On colour theory	07
Understanding undertones in paint colours	09
Sunny side up - Paris (FR)	10
The depth of blue - Rome (IT)	21
White with a bite - Bologna (IT)	30
Purple, gold, glittering and groovy - Milan (IT)	41
Green and red but make it sophisticated - Milan (IT)	48
A haven of serenity - Milan (IT)	57
Escape to warmer climates - Fontainebleau (FR)	64
Anything but square - New York (US)	73
A kaleidoscopic dream - Utrecht (NL)	80
Life in a technicolour classic - Wimbledon (UK)	91
Pink like red but not quite - Arezzo (IT)	100
Colour as an act of happiness - Paris (FR)	111
A colourful ode to Max Clendinning - Milan (IT)	118
Homage to the red lily of Florence - Florence (IT)	127
Nostalgic colours, clashing patterns - Milan (IT)	134
Reflections of Mount Vesuvius and the sea - Naples (IT)	143
Riding a pink cloud - Cape Town (SA)	152
Express yourself/don't repress yourself - Lyon (FR)	163
A white canvas packed with playfulness - Pelham (US)	172
Unconventional room with a view - Rio de Janeiro (BR)	183
Curious and curiouser - Henley (UK)	192
A marriage between vibrancy and subtlety - Aix-en-Provence (FR)	203
Primary colours under the eaves - Neuilly-Plaisance (FR)	212
Quirky curiosities, muted colours - Cape Town (SA)	221
Delivering the unexpected - London (UK)	230
Madness to the method - Milan (IT)	239
Orange is the new black - Turin (IT)	246
Thank you	254
Picture credits	255
Bibliography	255

ON CHOOSING COLOUR

You don't fully realise the impact of colour choices until you're decorating a house and want to dip your toes into the world of colour. Even I, after having painted and decorated my own homes, still find it difficult to choose the right colour for a space or object.

That's because colours don't exist in isolation – they interact with and are influenced by the hues around them. Yet, many people still try to choose colours remotely (yes, me too!). But what looks great in one space (or under the harsh strip lights of a paint shop) can appear completely different – or even terrible – elsewhere. To make the right choice, it's crucial to test your selected palette in the actual space you plan to paint, observing it at different times of the day to see how natural and artificial light and other colours surrounding it affect its appearance.

Colour theory in interior design is the understanding and application of principles that govern how colours interact with each other. Colour harmony refers to the visually pleasing arrangement of colours in a way that is balanced, cohesive, and captivating.

This book will help you find your footing and joy in the endless world of colours, offering plenty of inspiration on colour harmony. So go and strike a balance – or don't... because that's the fun of it!

ON
COLOUR
THEORY

If you divide the rainbow into three parts, you get red, yellow, and blue. Primary colours are made up of three pigments: red, yellow, and blue. They cannot be mixed or formed by any combination of any colour. But all other colours come from mixing these colours. Secondary colours are green, orange, and purple. These are formed by mixing the primary colours. The significance of secondary colours lies in their role as intermediate hues in the colour spectrum. Tertiary colours are yellow-orange, red-orange, red-purple, blue-purple, blue-green, and yellow-green. They are formed by mixing a primary colour and a secondary colour. This blending process results in a more nuanced and complex range of colours, adding depth and subtlety to the overall colour spectrum.

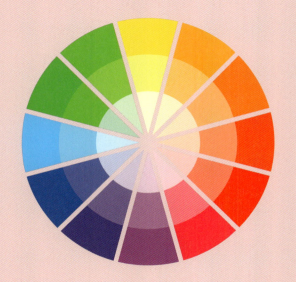

HUE, TINT, TONE, SHADE

Hue forms the outer edge of the colour wheel and refers directly to the colour name, like blue, yellow, or green. A hue is a colour in its purest form. And as they're pretty vivid (or saturated), they're often lightened, greyed, or darkened. A tint is a colour that has been diluted by the addition of white – making it lighter. It remains exactly the same colour, only a paler version. A tone (or value) is a colour to which grey has been added – neutralised or made greyer. It will tone down the intensity of any colour. A shade is a hue to which black has been added – to darken the original colour. It remains the same hue, only a darker version.

COLOUR SCHEMES (OR COLOUR HARMONY)

There are several types of colour schemes, each creating a different visual effect and mood in a space. Here's an overview.

→ A **MONOCHROMATIC** palette uses different shades, tints, and tones of a single colour, and creates a cohesive and harmonious look with subtle variations. For example, use various shades of blue for a calm and unified aesthetic.

MONOCHROMATIC

→ An **ANALOGOUS** colour scheme combines colours that are next to each other on the colour wheel (e.g., blue, blue-green, and green). It produces a natural and serene feel, often inspired by nature. The best approach is to pick one dominant colour and use the others as accents.

ANALOGOUS

→ A **COMPLEMENTARY** colour scheme pairs colours that are directly opposite each other on the colour wheel (e.g., blue and orange, red and green). This high contrast creates a bold and energetic look. Best used in moderation to avoid visual strain (or not, because it's your party, after all).

COMPLEMENTARY

→ A **SPLIT-COMPLEMENTARY** palette uses a base colour and two adjacent colours to its complementary (e.g., blue with yellow-orange and red-orange). This offers strong contrast while being slightly less intense than a direct complementary scheme. It's a balanced way to introduce vibrancy without overwhelming the space.

SPLIT COMPLEMENTARY

→ A **TRIADIC** colour arrangement involves three evenly spaced colours on the colour wheel (e.g., red, yellow, and blue) and creates a lively, high-contrast, dynamic statement. It works best when one colour dominates, and the others are used as accents.

TRIAD

→ A **TETRADIC** (double complementary) scheme uses two complementary colour pairs (e.g., blue and orange + red and green). It allows for a rich and varied palette but requires careful balancing. For optimal effect, pick one dominant colour with the others in supporting roles.

TETRAD

→ A **NEUTRAL** and **ACCENTED NEUTRAL** palette utilises neutral tones like white, grey, beige, or brown, often paired with a pop of colour. It provides a timeless and elegant base, while the accent colour adds interest. Versatile and adaptable across various styles.

SATURATION VS MUTED

Muted colours are those with low saturation, appearing softer and less intense. In contrast, saturated colours are highly vivid. A space where every piece of furniture is bright, and all walls are painted in saturated colours can feel overwhelming and chaotic. To create a more harmonious and visually balanced design, it's beneficial to incorporate muted colours alongside bright ones.

Muted colours are created by mixing a colour with its complementary counterpart from the colour wheel, resulting in a more neutralised colour. Unlike tints or shades, muted colours maintain a balanced depth. Another way to achieve muted colours is by blending colours with earthy hues, adding warmth and subtlety to a palette.

UNDERSTANDING UNDERTONES IN PAINT COLOURS

An undertone is the sneaky hint of colour hiding within your so-called 'neutral' paint choice – often revealing itself only after you've spent an entire weekend painting. If you've ever looked around a freshly painted room and wondered why it doesn't match your vision, mismatched undertones could be the culprit. By paying attention to undertones and lighting, you can avoid surprises and choose colours that look just as you envisioned.

WHAT ARE UNDERTONES?
Whenever a colour is created by mixing two or more colours, it has both a mass tone and an undertone. The mass tone is the first thing you see it tells you the colour is red, blue, green, and so on. The undertone, however, is what subtly influences how the colour appears. The closer the undertone is to the mass tone, the truer the colour will look. For example, a true red has a mass tone and undertone that are nearly identical. Magenta has a blue undertone. Poppy red has an orange undertone.

HOW TO SPOT AN UNDERTONE
Colours don't exist in isolation. A white wall might just look white until you place it next to a pure white. Suddenly, hints of green, pink, or blue emerge. You can use this trick with any colour. Compare your chosen colour to a pure version of that colour (a colour wheel can help). Check the darker shades of a hue if you have a drawdown paint swatch undertones are much easier to detect in deeper hues than in pale ones.

WARM VS. COOL UNDERTONES
Understanding a colour's temperature can help you choose the right shade for your space. Warm colours have undertones of orange, yellow, or red and create a cosy or energetic feel. Cool colours have undertones of green, blue, or purple and tend to feel fresh and soothing.

THE IMPACT OF LIGHTING
Natural and artificial light can dramatically shift how a colour appears. Northern light (cool, blue-toned) enhances blue undertones. Southern light (warm, golden) makes colours look creamier. Artificial lighting also plays a role incandescent bulbs (if you still have any) add warmth, while fluorescent lighting can bring out green or blue undertones. Energy-efficient dimmable LED lights allow you to adjust the intensity and colouring of your lighting and can also impact the way you experience a colour palette.

COLOUR COMBINATIONS SUNNY SIDE UP

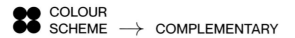

COLOUR SCHEME → COMPLEMENTARY

Yellow has long been a colour of contrasts, symbolising both decay and lawlessness as well as value and beauty. Yet, when used in the interior, whether as an accent or a dominant colour, it brings warmth and energy, making it an undeniably gorgeous and joyous choice. Yellow creates rooms that are rich and enveloping, like a warm embrace.

SUNNY SIDE UP

Nestled on a charming street in Paris's XVIIe Arrondissement, amidst early 20th-century architecture, lies the vibrant 70-square-metre apartment of creative partners Alice Gras and Anaïs Seguin. This colourful, joyful space radiates creativity and good humour while preserving a tranquil ambience.

Yellow, chosen for its uplifting qualities of joy, good humour, cheerfulness, and warmth, takes centre stage, perfectly complementing their light-filled open space. The kitchen and bathroom underwent substantial renovations, resonating with memories of travels and family traditions. Inspired by the graphic allure of Southern France, Alice designed the boldly geometric and contemporary tiles of the kitchen floor herself.

Alice and Anaïs cleverly chose a lighter shade of yellow for the kitchen, combined with an overall monochrome palette for a more earthy aesthetic. This creates a subdued, cosy feel – always important for spaces where you spend a lot of time. That said, make sure you use natural light to select the right shade of yellow.

In north-facing rooms, you want to bounce light around, so stick to bright yellows and stay away from green or blue undertones. Light in south-facing rooms becomes warmer, meaning deep yellows will be intensified. In that case, maybe try a warm sand or rich ochre for a more subtle effect. If you don't want to paint all your walls yellow, pair it with a muted colour, like white or grey. Or introduce a bold colour with a dash of blue.

In their purest, primary-colour forms, yellow and blue are often used to stand out, especially in creating memorable logos (the big blue Swedish brand comes to mind). However, these bold characteristics don't always translate into a harmonious home. Blue and yellow are opposites on the colour wheel, each bringing distinct qualities to a space. While blue exudes tranquillity and seriousness, yellow radiates joy and energy. Yet, the residents skilfully balance these contrasting hues, allowing blue to dominate in the separate dining room, where it's paired with calming white. The white walls are accented by colourful artwork, making the blue dining room a serene focal point that perfectly balances the vibrant yellow. The warm wooden tones of the floor blend seamlessly with both yellow and blue, tying the space together. For the bedroom, Alice and Anaïs drew inspiration from a hotel photo and wanted a distinctive, adaptable headboard. Some old sheets, once belonging to a great-grandmother, were perfect for the look they envisioned, so they carefully and painstakingly marked the pleats and created a beautiful headboard. The soothing sea blue, pale yellow, soft greens, and greys echo the palette of the rest of the apartment, creating an inviting, calm haven where the residents can unwind and relax.

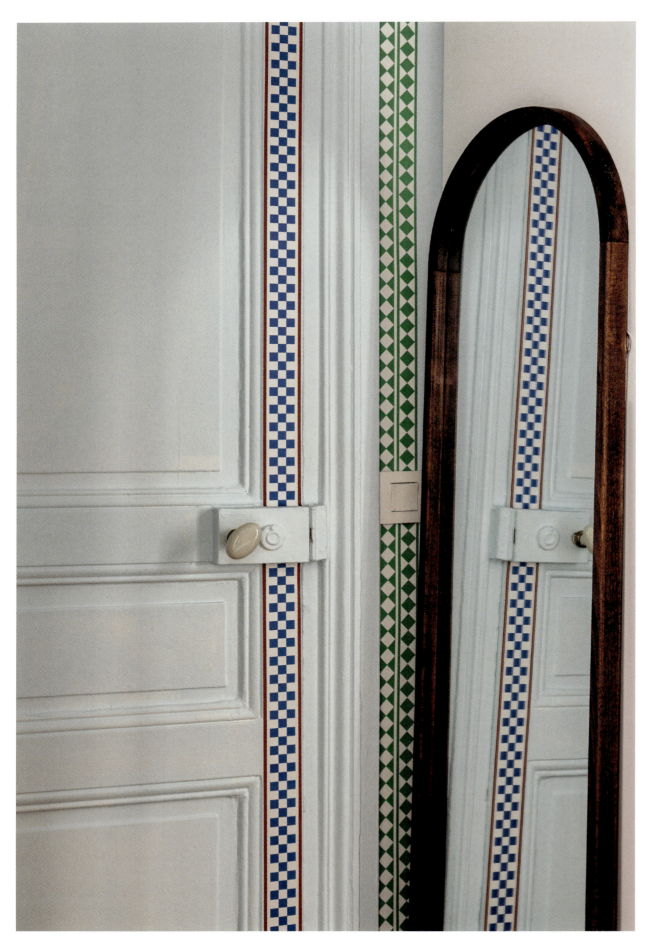

SUNNY SIDE UP

COLOUR COMBINATIONS

Injecting black hues into a yellow room brings balance into the space and elevates the level of sophistication.

THE DEPTH OF BLUE   COLOUR COMBINATIONS

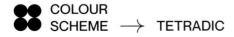
COLOUR SCHEME → TETRADIC

In ancient Egypt, blue symbolised the sky, the River Nile, creation, and divinity. In Europe, however, blue didn't carry such significant associations until the 12th century. At that time, a French abbot declared blue hues divine, and artists began depicting the Virgin Mary in ultramarine, marking the start of the colour's positive connotations. Ask a random person nowadays what their favourite colour is, and chances are the answer will be blue.

COLOUR THEORY

THE DEPTH OF BLUE

Giorgia Cerulli and Giacomo Guidi, a couple in both work and life, prioritised finding a quiet space to unwind at the end of the day. Eventually, they fell in love with the details of their perfectly preserved 140-square-metre 1950s apartment in Rome's San Saba neighbourhood.

The high stuccoed ceilings, original windows, and especially the polychrome floors – each room featuring unique flooring patterns like Palladian, stripes, zigzags, graphic tiles, and parquet – were the true highlights. Preserving the apartment's excellent condition, they merely removed a few doors and painted the walls a rich dark blue, eliminating the vintage patina common in older homes. Giorgia chose cobalt and blue bone china as dominant colours – hues that change during the day and that remind her of the soft sea foam of Sabaudia, a beloved Roman holiday spot of hers. The dramatic cobalt blue serves as a stunning backdrop, enhancing complementary hues like orange, purple, and yellow. All that was left was to add furniture, objects, and artworks.

Half-painted walls are a brilliant way of injecting colour into your home and a good compromise between coloured and white walls. Instead of a traditional half-and-half division, Giorgia and Giacomo opted for a reversed split, leaving the top third of the wall unpainted. This design choice adds an element of surprise and grandeur. Horizontal lines make any room appear wider and more spacious.

THE DEPTH OF BLUE

COLOUR COMBINATIONS

THE DEPTH OF BLUE

COLOUR COMBINATIONS

Using a dark blue shade on the lower part of the wall and a tinted white tone above makes these rooms feel both spacious and light. Since white tones also have different nuances, make sure that your white is tinted with undertones that harmonise with the lower colour. It is, by the way, best to paint the ceiling the same colour as the upper wall area. This creates less contrast, causing the boundary between the wall and ceiling to blur.

Blue's versatility allows it to feel both timeless and contemporary. It's ideal when seeking something dark but softer than black. Painting walls and ceilings in the same inky shade also blurs the boundaries between areas, creating the illusion of a larger space.

A warm shade, like yellow or brown, can counteract the coolness of blue and highlight its warmer undertones. These shades don't need to match perfectly – casually combining different hues and patterns, such as the beautiful flooring and wooden furniture, adds intriguing layers to the overall design. Paired with neutrals, it achieves a classic and enduring look. Use it as a focal point (see pages 12–19) or add drama by colour drenching (see pages 102–109) a north-facing room in a rich shade of navy.

The pink bathroom off the hall provides a break from the blue, making it feel both spacious and light.

COLOUR COMBINATIONS   WHITE WITH A BITE

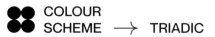

COLOUR
SCHEME → TRIADIC

From the coloured chalk used in the earliest surviving cave art to the vibrant aesthetics of Miami Vice, pastels are far more dynamic than their simple, understated reputation suggests. Pastels can be both edgy and intriguing, offering contrasts while remaining warm, soft, and bright. After some decades of silence, pastel colours broke back into mainstream interior design in the early 2000s, shedding their last traces of tameness.

WHITE WITH A BITE

COLOUR COMBINATIONS

WHITE WITH A BITE

The discovery of an ancient fresco in their 100-square-metre apartment, housed in a 19th-century Bologna building, served as inspiration for designers and partners Andres Eduardo Avanzi and Martina Vesco. Their design exemplifies a sophisticated take on the subdued, pale variations of the bold colours found on the colour wheel.

The renovation of the apartment took six months. Every design and stylistic decision was carefully examined and approved by a city commission for the superintendence of fine arts, as the entire building is under its protection. The only structural intervention was the creation of openings on both sides of the corridor that once separated the living room from the kitchen. This modification effectively doubled the proportions of the living area. The high ceilings, soaring over 3.3 metres, further enhance the sense of verticality, a feeling echoed by the custom-designed, full-height kitchen.

Andres and Martina know their pastels and created a scheme that is anything but bland. It was the faint blue, glimpsed beneath the layers of paint and plaster during their apartment renovation, that set them on their pastel-coloured interior path – for they suspected it was an original fresco. After hours of careful work, the fresco was revealed, forming the foundation for the apartment's colour scheme: light blues, warm yellows, soft pinks, and greens, reflected in materials, finishes, furniture, and lighting.

WHITE WITH A BITE

COLOUR COMBINATIONS

WHITE WITH A BITE

COLOUR COMBINATIONS

The white window frames enhance the sense of openness and airiness, reflecting natural light throughout the space.

The off-white walls and wooden floors create a neutral base, while the lively patterns on the rugs beautifully elevate the subdued palette. The rough, frescoed wall in the dining room complements the overall scheme of the space and adds a delicious grunginess to it. It is literally rough around the edges. Also notice the refined black details that are used. Combining pastels with black is like a biker stepping into a florist's studio – it creates a striking and unexpected contrast.

    Many people mistakenly opt for brilliant white when painting their walls. While it can look stunning in the warm glow of summer sunlight, it often falls short during darker, gloomier days, reflecting that same grey and dull tone back into the space.

Instead, consider off-whites or a soft linen or sand tone. Pastels not only add colour but also create visual calm. These hues provide a subtle warmth and are often easier to integrate into a cohesive design scheme. Keep in mind that a colour can vary not only from room to room or due to lighting, but it can also look different depending on the other surfaces in the space. The green you love might not look great next to bright white but could work beautifully next to an off-white with the right undertone. One coloured wall next to a bright white wall creates a stark contrast, making the wall stand out quite a lot. If you paint one wall pink and the rest in a warm white or sand tone, the contrast is much softer, resulting in a much subtler effect.

38

WHITE WITH A BITE

COLOUR COMBINATIONS

PURPLE, GOLD, GLITTERING AND GROOVY — COLOUR COMBINATIONS

COLOUR SCHEME → **SPLIT-COMPLEMENTARY**

Purple has long been associated with power and wealth, thanks to the challenging, costly, and rather unpleasant process – especially for the sea snails from which it was derived – of creating the first purple dye, Tyrian purple. Combining the calming qualities of blue with the warmth of red, purple is incredibly versatile. It's a colour people either love or hate, perhaps because of its bold and commanding personality.

PURPLE, GOLD, GLITTERING AND GROOVY

Located in a 1940s building in a lively neighbourhood of Milan, Martina Castoldi's apartment has been given a colourful touch by architect Piergiorgio Fasoli. Together, they selected the colours, upholstery, furnishings, and lamps that define each room's character. The result is perfect synergy – a reflection of the personality of the architect as well as the client.

Piergiorgio redefined the spaces of what was once an office, transforming it into a large corner living room with three windows, a dining area, a kitchen, and a bar counter, all in vibrant colours. For a bold approach, purple combined with bright shades like heliotrope, violet, gold, hot pink, and verdigris produces a striking, maximalist décor, as showcased in this interior. The objects within the space come from various eras and contexts – great-grandmother's sideboards, ultra-modern design pieces, art and philosophy books, and vibrant porcelain treasures from market finds – all coexisting with purpose.

The maximalist interior, striking a balance between a temple and a groovy club, feels like a shot of adrenaline coursing through your veins. Everything in this house has been executed on a grand scale, from the 1980s gold-toned bar to the architraves (inspired by the façade and common areas of the building) above the doorways and the tiles in the bathroom. Its personality gleams and glistens, greeting you with a grand gesture.

The colour palette has also been approached on a grand scale. Grand and well-thought-out.

PURPLE, GOLD, GLITTERING AND GROOVY

COLOUR COMBINATIONS

In the hallway, a brightly patterned black wallpaper is paired with a warm yellow, offering a beautiful contrast that highlights the vibrant jackets on the coat rack.

By painting the walls in shades of heliotrope and Baker-Miller pink, a softer contrast is created, providing the perfect backdrop for other, more vibrant colours. The verdigris green (or copper-green) ceiling brims with energy, complementing the overall energetic feel of the space. The purple shades teamed with soft magenta velvets are the perfect finisher – the combination oozes sophistication and luxury. Gold, as a yellow colour, is complementary to purple. By adding gold and brass details to the interior, Martina and Piergiorgio created an opulent, bold look.

Black works beautifully with strong jewel tones and the bath- or cloakroom may be the perfect place to start out with it. In the powder room, deep smoky eggplant and black create a sense of mystery and elegance, establishing a mood that is both enchanting and sophisticated, and brimful of personality.

If you love purple as much as Martina but want to use a more toned-down version, neutralise purple by choosing a tone of soft purple and combining it with an off-white or linen. Deep purples paired with complementary tones like olive green, chartreuse, or ochre create a more traditional look.

PURPLE, GOLD, GLITTERING AND GROOVY

COLOUR COMBINATIONS

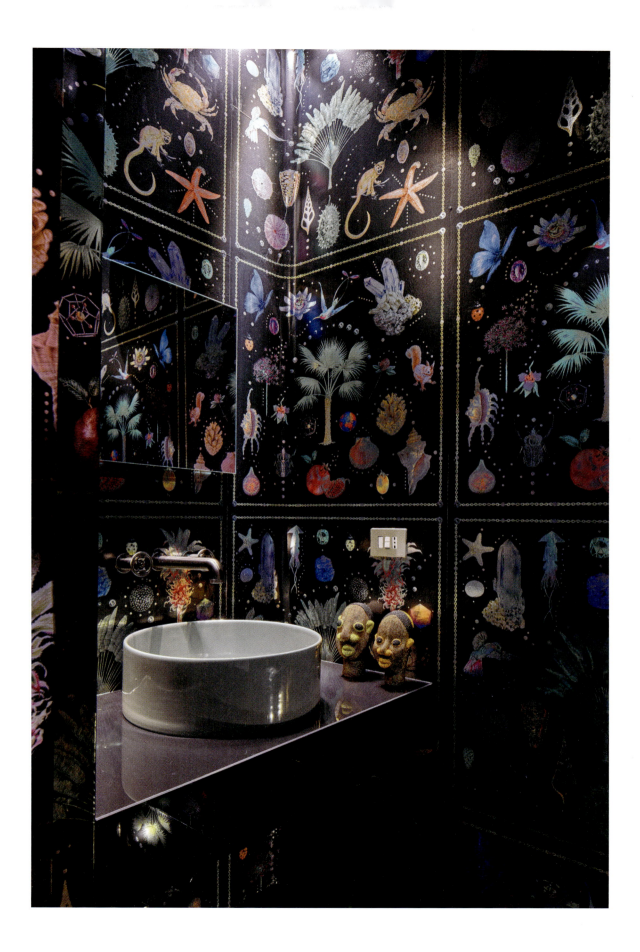

COLOUR COMBINATIONS	GREEN AND RED BUT MAKE IT SOPHISTICATED

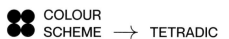

COLOUR SCHEME → TETRADIC

Maybe you have fond memories of junior school, maybe you don't... but one thing is certain: your school memories are likely drenched in the primary colours blue, yellow, and red. Primary and secondary colours have an inherent playfulness and mood-boosting quality and incorporating them into your interior is a rebellion against restrained, super serious colour schemes.

GREEN AND RED BUT MAKE IT SOPHISTICATED

COLOUR COMBINATIONS

GREEN AND RED BUT MAKE IT SOPHISTICATED

Gaia Venuti's home is located in a converted 1940s factory next to the Darsena and Navigli district, close to the Milan city centre. For 20 years, it has been her playground and has seen many changes – the right place for continuous experimentation and surprising (colour) combinations.

The 90-square-metre apartment is on the second floor of the building and features an open space with a kitchen and living room, plus two bedrooms. According to Gaia, a former fashion accessories designer turned interior designer, designing a home feels much like putting together an outfit. You start with a palette and then build a mood around it. Right now, her inspiration comes from the fabulous 1970s, blending vintage Italian and Nordic furnishings sourced from second-hand dealers or patiently hunted down in markets.

With their high saturation, primary colours work best as sub-dominant or accent hues in interior design. Pair them with soft neutrals or earthy tones – like Gaia did with butter yellow walls – to create a balanced backdrop that highlights vibrant pops of colour. Although grey is often considered a safe choice, the kitchen demonstrates its potential for sophistication when combined with bright hues, providing contrast and visual interest. When using primary colours alongside neutrals, also consider texture. Natural materials such as wool, linen, and wood add warmth to the design and soften the boldness of the bright hues, creating a balanced and inviting atmosphere. The kitchen rug, an eye-catching piece reminiscent of a Jackson Pollock masterpiece, looks so enticing you almost want to sink your teeth into it.

It also mirrors the colours of the living area next to it, tying both spaces perfectly together. The living area features refined design pieces paired with gorgeous green curtains, repurposed from old upholstery drapes, giving them a fresh new character.

Anyone who thinks the colour combination of red and green is reserved solely for the wardrobe of Christmas elves or holiday decorations has yet to encounter the pairing of emerald green (or 'Gaia-green' as she likes to call it – it's a colour created by a painter just for her) and reddish-brown, as shown in the bedroom. Suddenly, the combination becomes refined and sophisticated, far removed from any association with gnomes or Christmas trees.

To prevent primary colours from overwhelming rather than enhancing a space, achieving the right balance is key when incorporating them into a room. The 60–30–10 rule of choosing colour can help you come up with a harmonious interior colour scheme. It states that 60 per cent of the room (floor, walls – ceiling included – and big pieces of furniture) should be in a dominant colour, 30 per cent (curtains, rugs, smaller pieces of furniture) in a secondary colour or texture, and the last 10 per cent (art, decoration, floor cushions, etc.) should be in an accent colour.

The swathes and small accessories of bright red bring another level of richness to the earthy base.

GREEN AND RED BUT MAKE IT SOPHISTICATED

COLOUR COMBINATIONS

GREEN AND RED BUT MAKE IT SOPHISTICATED

COLOUR COMBINATIONS

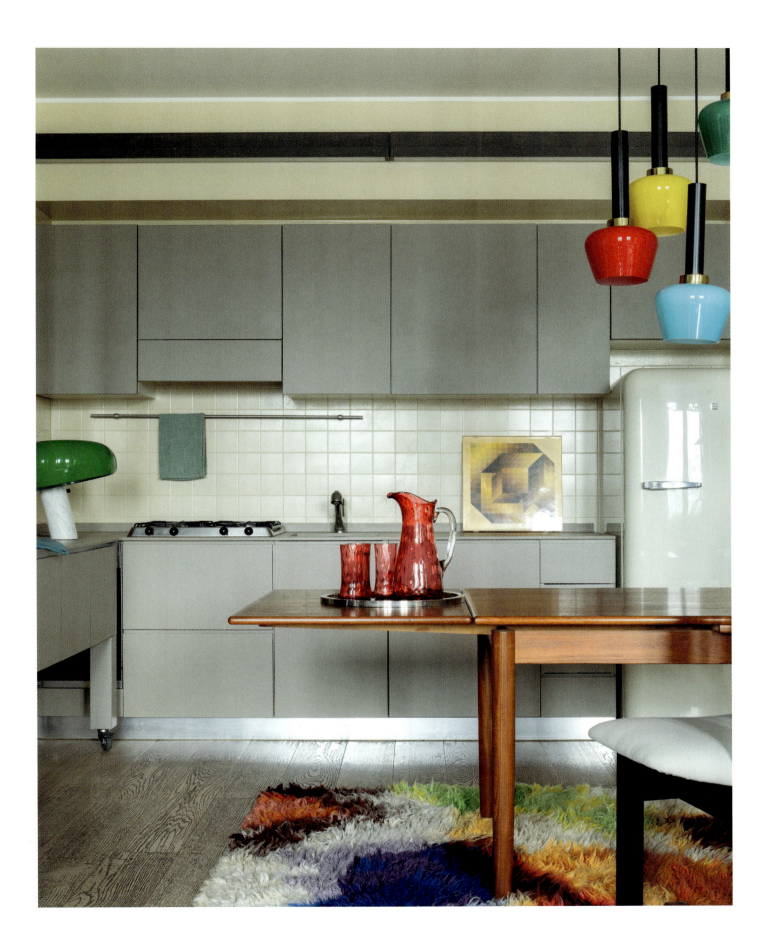

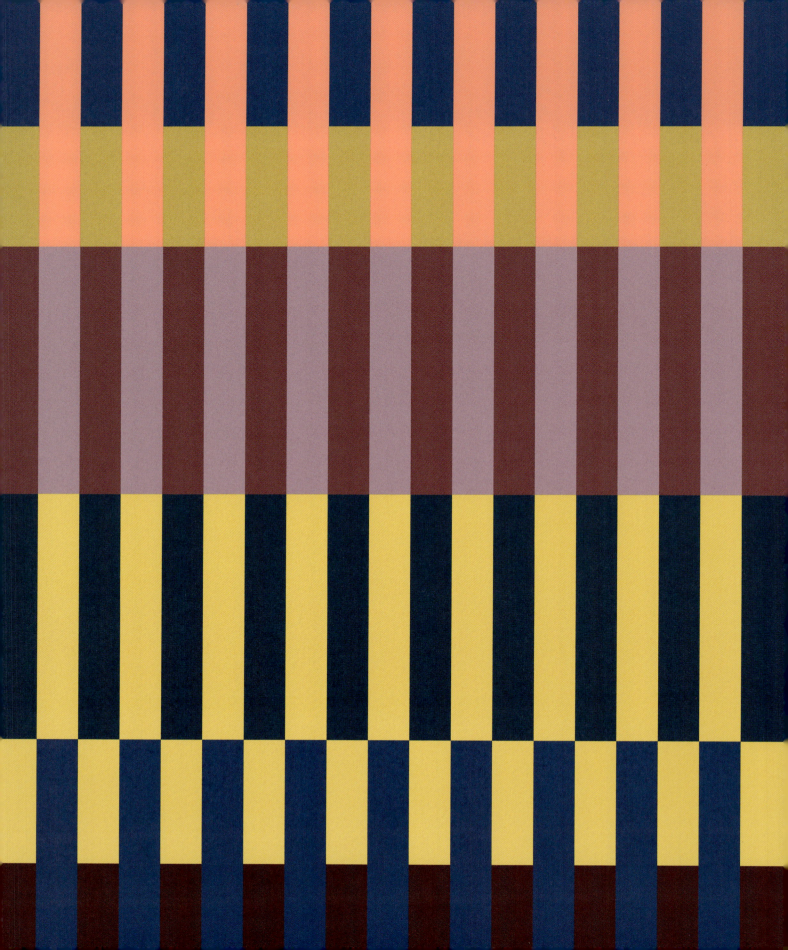

A HAVEN OF SERENITY　　　　　　　　　　　　　　　　　　　　　　　　COLOUR COMBINATIONS

COLOUR SCHEME → SPLIT-COMPLEMENTARY

Gold symbolises not only luxury and elegance, but also greed and envy. The dual nature of gold is perhaps best illustrated by the story of the mythical King Midas, who was granted the ability to turn everything he touched into gold – while initially a joy, the gift soon became a curse, preventing him from eating or drinking. The secret Midas discovered – that adding glints of gold prevents things from becoming lacklustre – applies equally to gold in interior design.

A HAVEN OF SERENITY

The location of the pied-à-terre (a skyscraper) and the colour of dusk – when the day transitions into night and the sky fills with blue –served as the inspiration for the interior design of this Milanese pied-à-terre, created by Daniele Daminelli.

Daniele's design became a true sanctuary, a place to retreat from the chaos and observe the lively city from a distance – like an ivory tower that shields and embraces its inhabitants. When night falls, the interior and exterior of the space seamlessly connect, enveloping its inhabitants in a serene atmosphere, accentuated by its tranquil Chinoiserie details.

In the main space, the wallpaper offers a beautiful contrast to the surrounding environment. It introduces a decorative element that contrasts with the building's minimalism. Daniele's goal was to incorporate an oriental influence – not necessarily tied to geography, but to the romanticism this style of decoration is associated with. In a distinctly minimal space, such ornamentation serves as a beautiful merging of styles. A contemporary photographer's Caravaggio-esque images of modern-day motifs complete the space's colour palette and tranquil atmosphere.

A HAVEN OF SERENITY

COLOUR COMBINATIONS

> Daniele incorporated the gold from the wallpaper into the lamps – a clever way to create unity.

Glossy finishes, such as shiny fabrics, high-gloss paint and glass complete the feel of elegance and glamour. Daniele let rich colours and textures shine by opting for plush velvet and chenille for upholstery and soft furnishings. All these reflective surfaces enhance natural light, brightening the space and creating a sense of openness. Dark hues add contrast, making the shiny accents stand out even more. Dark shades don't necessarily make a room look stuffy or overcrowded. When paired with minimalist principles, they create a serene, sophisticated atmosphere. Keep the design simple but luxurious, avoiding excessive ornamentation. As you can see, a single beautiful autumn branch in a simple vase makes a striking, sculptural arrangement.

From its use in ancient palaces and temples to its modern-day prominence in diverse decorative styles, gold transcends trends. Gold's versatility extends beyond its ability to complement various materials and textures – it also pairs effortlessly with a range of colours. Soft pastels, deep jewel tones, and earthy neutrals all work well with gold. For example, gold accents with royal blues and reds evoke richness – as shown here – while gold with blush tones creates a romantic feel (see pages 82–89). This adaptability makes gold suitable for diverse interior styles, even minimalist and timeless Scandinavian designs, where it adds warmth and sophistication in neutral spaces.

A HAVEN OF SERENITY

COLOUR COMBINATIONS

COLOUR COMBINATIONS   ESCAPE TO WARMER CLIMATES

COLOUR SCHEME → ANALOGOUS

A 2017 study by scientists at the Massachusetts Institute of Technology (MIT) shows that languages tend to divide the warm part of the colour spectrum into more colour words compared to the cool parts. This could be explained by the fact that human vision is adapted to perceive warmer colours as closer due to their higher energy and visibility in various lighting conditions. In short, when you apply rich, earthy tones to your interior, it will embrace you like the warmest, cosiest sweater you've ever owned.

ESCAPE TO WARMER CLIMATES

The area around Fontainebleau, southeast of Paris, is home to one of France's largest national forests, making it a beloved weekend retreat for Parisians. Since the 19th century, it has also drawn numerous impressionist artists, including self-taught decorative artist Victor Cadene.

Victor, known for his use of colour and passion for decorative arts, which he showcases in his warm, dreamy home, creates two-dimensional scenes from his drawings, which he cuts out and assembles into collages. Much of his work is scattered throughout his old house in the pretty village of Bourron-Marlotte. The original structure of the building remained largely unchanged, except for the kitchen and bathroom, both of which have been fully renovated. The many subtle interventions throughout the space are a testament to Victor's creative vision, whose drawings were initially a means of expression for his interior design projects. It's clear that both the owner's life and work – inseparable from one another – are equally shaped by their owner's travels, encounters, and a collection of objects rich with history.

The contrasting white ceiling and bedsheets cut through the darker shades for a fresh feel.

Even on the coldest, gloomiest day of the year, the sun seems to shine in Victor's home. Burnt orange, shades of deep olive, burgundy and ochre give these rooms interest and balance without being overpowering. The chosen palette – reminiscent of old ceramic pots, colourful tile roofs, sun-kissed ochre façades and the surrounding forests – creates a warm, inviting atmosphere. The Terre verte (or Verona green) walls in the living room, a colour originating from Mediterranean regions like Cyprus and Verona, further enhance this warm feel.

A celadon-coloured ceiling (as seen in Victor's dining room) adds unexpected contrast – rich textures and layered materials infuse more character and charm. Victor often emphasises texture, especially within toned-down or analogous colour schemes. As this colour palette does not compete, it makes it an excellent foundation for bold and grand interior gestures. The curvaceous green velvet sofa, artisan-glazed ceramic stool, and wall drawings (also created by Victor) elevate the earthy backdrop to a beautiful timeless whole, packed with character.

Beware of the risk of drenching a home entirely in earthy neutrals, as it can make the space feel dull. Adding vibrant browns and oranges can tip the scales toward a groovy 1970s vibe that might not make you feel entirely comfortable either. You avoid both by adding contrasting tones or shades of oranges, browns, and reds – the mature versions of their bright counterparts.

ANYTHING BUT SQUARE COLOUR COMBINATIONS

COLOUR SCHEME → TRIADIC

Originally at home in the art world – particularly in the works of Piet Mondrian and other modernist painters – colour blocking eventually found its way into our homes. Colour blocking means choosing contrasting colour combinations that stand out from each other but still harmonise. Choosing hues from the outer edges of the colour wheel creates a deliciously strong contrast that energises and enlivens a space.

COLOUR THEORY

ANYTHING

BUT SQUARE

This 1954 house in upstate New York was literally constructed from a kit and is, according to its owner, industrial designer Karim Rashid, more of an industrial product than a work of architecture. All the components were made in a factory and assembled on-site in just six days.

Located just a five-minute walk uphill from the Scarborough train station, Karim and his wife Megan, a digital artist whose cyber graffiti adorns much of the house's walls, bought the property online in September 2001 after only seeing 360-degree webcam photos of it. Two months later, they were taken by surprise when the surrounding trees shed their leaves, revealing a large shopping mall just behind the house. Looking back, they now see it as a fortunate discovery. They do all their grocery shopping at that mall.

Before Karim and Megan applied their signature style to it, the house had only two previous owners, both passionate about preservation. They maintained much of the original interior, including the kitchen cupboards, original colours, and even the paint pots for touching up the blue, lime, purple, and red walls. They also took colour blocking to an advanced level by highlighting interesting architectural features like the pillars in the living room.

Karim's bright home is filled with his own creations: soft, curling shapes bursting with colour. This isn't just because it makes the designs super-huggable and joyous; it also has a practical side. Since he broke his toe on a marble coffee table, he has developed an allergy to furniture with right angles. In addition to breaking up the straight lines of the house, there's something else that brings a great sense of joy to the interior: its bold colours. It's a misconception that vibrant colours are reserved solely for children's rooms. As children, our world is curated to be full of colour and playfulness. What rulebook says you have to drape your home in grey or white as soon as you grow up? Of course, joy is in the eye of the beholder, but Karim's unapologetically playful home shows how much vivid blues, vivacious reds, and warm yellows enliven a space. What I mean to say is: you never have to grow up when it comes to colour.

There are links between the colours we see and what we feel. So first, pick a single tone that makes your heart sing, whether it's a primary blue or yellow, a secondary fuchsia or bright orange. Once you've decided on your main colour, decide on the palette that will accompany it. Go for contrast like Karim did, or pick pared-back shades or even pastels for a softer effect (see pages 232–237). Or choose furniture in colours that clash or contrast to make the space feel bright and happy. Use the colour wheel to help you plan. And continually ask yourself: does this bring me joy? If it does, grab that bucket of red paint and unleash your inner child. Create an interior bursting with personality, not a place that looks like it could belong to anyone.

Silver, steel or other shiny accents create eye catching details – especially in a bold interior design.

ANYTHING BUT SQUARE

COLOUR COMBINATIONS

COLOUR COMBINATIONS   A KALEIDOSCOPIC DREAM

COLOUR SCHEME → TRIADIC

Surrealism emerged as an artistic movement in the early 20th century, led by figures like Dalí, Magritte, and Gaudí. Initially it found its expression primarily in art, while later its influence extended to interior design. Unconventional colour palettes that defy traditional norms, mesmerising patterns and surrealist furnishings offer a way to break free from the ordinary – allowing you to express your personality, creativity, and imagination within the confines of your home.

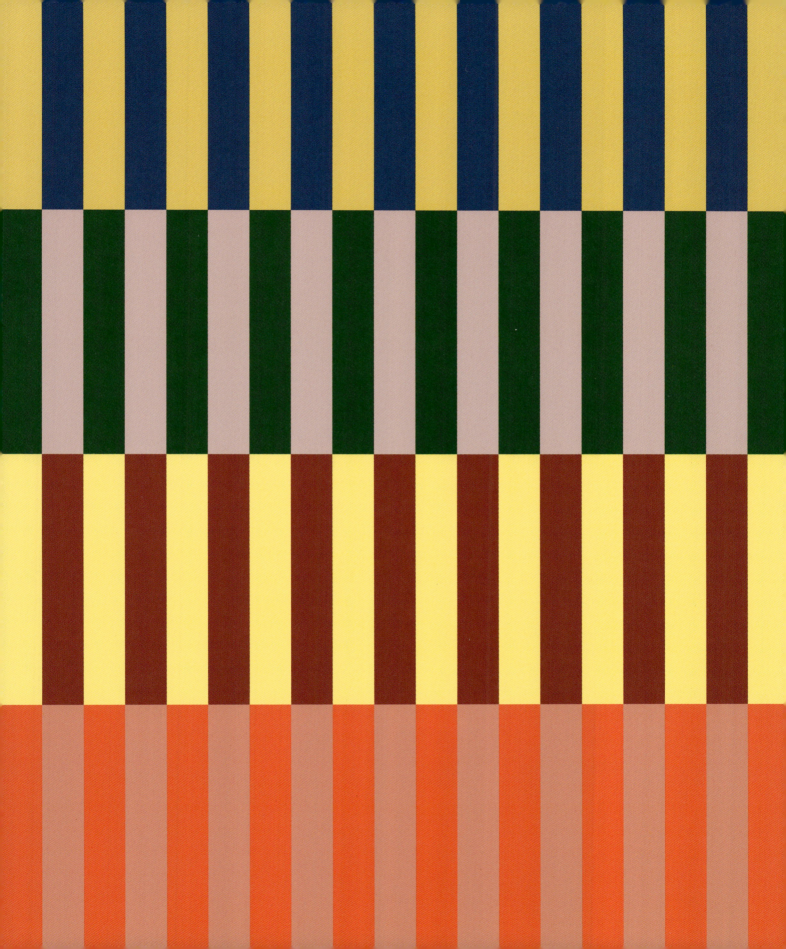

A KALEIDOSCOPIC DREAM

COLOUR COMBINATIONS

A KALEIDOSCOPIC DREAM

Dutch interior designer Sandra Planken reimagined a late 19th-century Utrecht canal house, once a flute factory, into a celebration of ironic, unconventional living – where antiques, avant-garde design, and clashing colours merge in a kaleidoscopic, sophisticated aesthetic.

Glowing like a sunset, a golden door pierces a crimson wall, reflecting the light that floods through the large windows. A fluorescent fuchsia palm leans against a 19th-century fireplace adorned with kaleidoscopic wallpaper. Nearby, an acid green bar table and stools by artist Jólan van der Wiel stand before an 1800s cupboard transformed into a bar. The vibrant scene includes the iconic Vilbert chair and old shutters painted in fire engine red, all clashing magnificently in surreal harmony – reminiscent of a Salvador Dalí painting.

With an unorthodox design, the building rises across three main floors, plus a basement offering direct access to the Oudegracht quay, the canal running through the heart of Utrecht's city centre. Sandra's goal was to remove traces of a 1980s renovation and restore the building's original features, including coffered ceilings and leaded stained-glass windows. The only piece retained from that era was a Versace velvet sofa discovered in the basement.

Of course, you can conduct extensive research into the history of your house and decorate it in the colours that were common at that time. Retaining and showcasing a building's unique architectural details and craftsmanship not only honours its heritage but also fosters a sense of authenticity and timelessness. However, incorporating rich colour palettes and vintage design elements with a modern twist creates a living space that bridges past, present, and personality. Colour (albeit on furniture) can be reversed and changed, removing architectural elements... not so much. So embrace those old architectural elements, respect their history, but shake things up with grand colourful gestures.

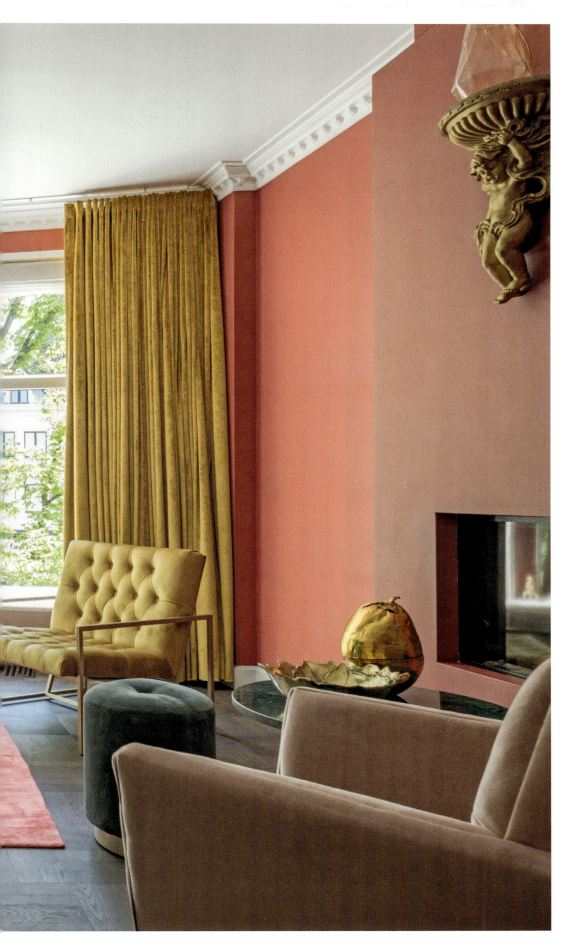

A KALEIDOSCOPIC DREAM

COLOUR COMBINATIONS

A KALEIDOSCOPIC DREAM

COLOUR COMBINATIONS

> The chequered wallpaper reflects in the opposite mirror, making both walls belong together.

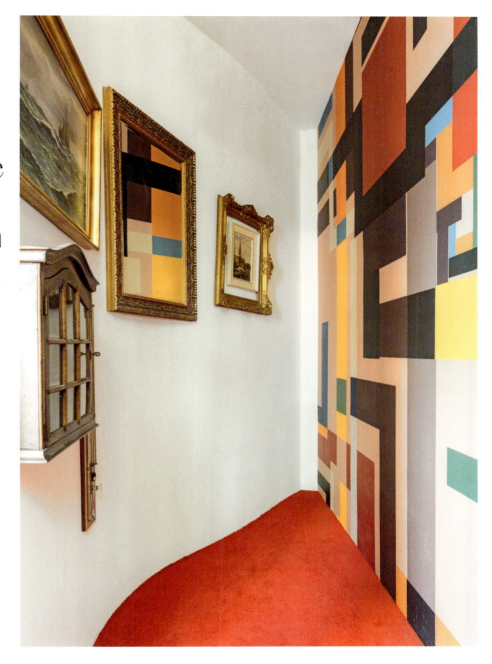

You can create your own original (or unconventional) colour scheme for your home by using what I would like to call echo colour theory. It involves using repeated hues throughout a space to create a harmonious, echo-like effect. While the intensity of the colours may vary, they all belong to the same colour palette, much like echoes of the same sound at different volumes. Also much like what happens when you turn a kaleidoscope. The pinks and greens of the dining room are echoed in the furnishings, while the flowerpots complement the wallpaper above the fireplace. The silver fridge is reflected in the floor and bar, and the red shutters are mirrored in the living room in a radicchio hue. The green spatulated wall complements the red, creating a harmonious colour palette. The result is a striking, colour-coordinated space that balances dynamic energy with unity.

LIFE IN A TECHNICOLOUR CLASSIC — COLOUR COMBINATIONS

COLOUR SCHEME → SPLIT-COMPLEMENTARY

In the wake of the sombre post-war years in the mid-20th century, a vibrant revolution known as pop art erupted onto the world of art and interior. The emergence of new and affordable acrylic paints played a crucial role in allowing pop artists to explore a broader spectrum of colours, contributing to the movement's bold aesthetic. This also meant that more bold and saturated colours entered our homes… and hearts.

COLOUR THEORY

LIFE IN A TECHNICOLOUR CLASSIC

Only the size of this single-storey Wimbledon house, built in the late 1960s, is modest. Designed by British-Italian architect Richard Rogers (1933-2021), the house itself is not only a model of cheerfulness and progressiveness, it also served as inspiration for Rogers's later world-famous work, the Centre Pompidou – the grand national centre for art and culture in the historical heart of Paris.

House Rogers – designed by Richard Rogers for his parents – is a landmark of post-war British architecture. The single-storey modernist house is made from bright, yellow-painted steel ribs with full-height glazing at each end and is separated into two parts. The experimental design combines prefabricated elements with integrated furniture, merging Californian modernism – emphasising harmony between home, landscape, and framed views through windows – with the adaptability of high-tech industrial systems. The bright yellow frame and vibrant interior colours defied Britain's drab domestic norms, reflecting Richard Rogers's Italian upbringing, his mother's pottery, his parents' collection of paintings by Ben Nicholson and other modern British masters, and their collection of iconic Eames and Ernesto Rogers furniture.

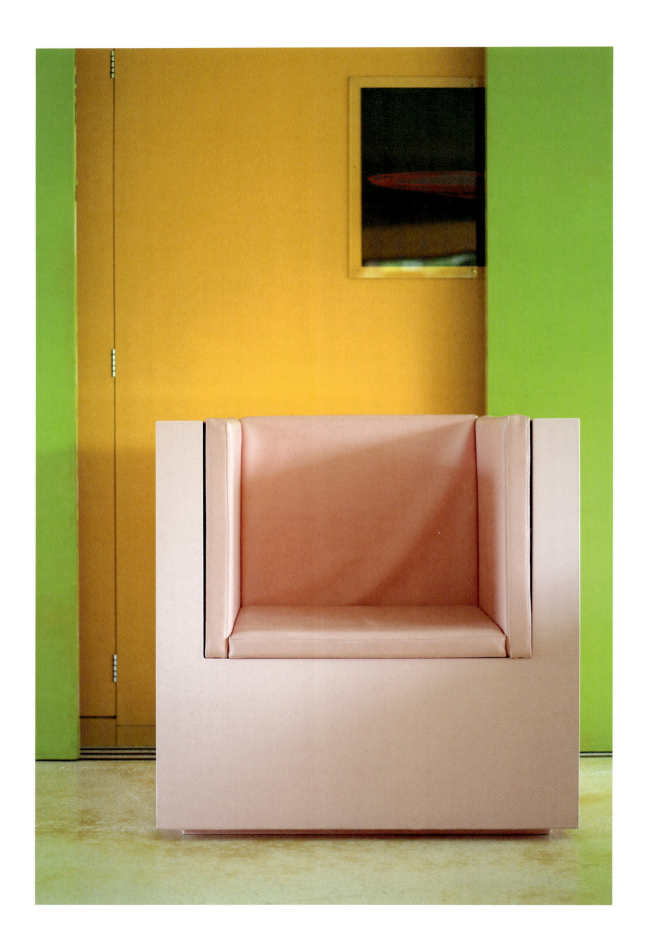

LIFE IN A TECHNICOLOUR CLASSIC

COLOUR COMBINATIONS

> Pink pairs beautifully with green, brown, golden yellow, grey or lilac once a child's pink phase comes to an end.

But it's not just the architecture that makes this house stand out. Rogers had a love for colour and famously avoided grey in his buildings. Looking at this house and its colours, it's almost unimaginable that the house is nearly 60 years old and that not all houses around the world look like this. Who wants to live in a brown brick box if this can be the alternative? For Richard Rogers, colour was fundamental – not only to differentiate the functions of various components using vibrant industrial paints but also as a way to convey pure joy. Think sunny yellow, saffron, hot pink, and what we now call brat green. You can bring these colours into your home with something as simple as a brightly coloured wall or as bold as an iconic multi-coloured piece of furniture – or both, if you're aiming for a cohesive look.

A single wall painted in a colour that doesn't appear anywhere else will stand out as an isolated object that doesn't relate to the rest of the space. When you repeat the colour in different places (or echo them – see pages 82–89), you enhance the overall look of your interior, creating a balanced ambience. Paint a wall in a contrasting colour or paint a cabinet in a bold colour (bright colours are great for upcycling furniture) and echo that colour in an armchair, a few accessories, such as cushions, vases, lampshades, or the blinds – as seen in House Rogers. By repeating colours, you create a cohesive feel in a room. Of course, you don't have to use the brightest version of the colour all the time, just incorporate different shades, such as a pastel pink chair, a fluorescent pink chair, and a shocking pink couch.

COLOUR COMBINATIONS　　　　PINK LIKE RED BUT NOT QUITE

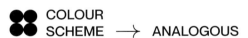

COLOUR SCHEME → ANALOGOUS

Interestingly, the pink-for-girls and blue-for-boys rule in Western societies is a mere century old. Before that, the colours were reversed: pink, a faded red, was associated with cardinals and uniforms, while blue was linked to the Virgin Mary. Because of its long-running cultural association with young girls and the feminine in general, pink can nowadays still be a tad divisive. And it is high time to reclaim it for spaces shared by all sexes.

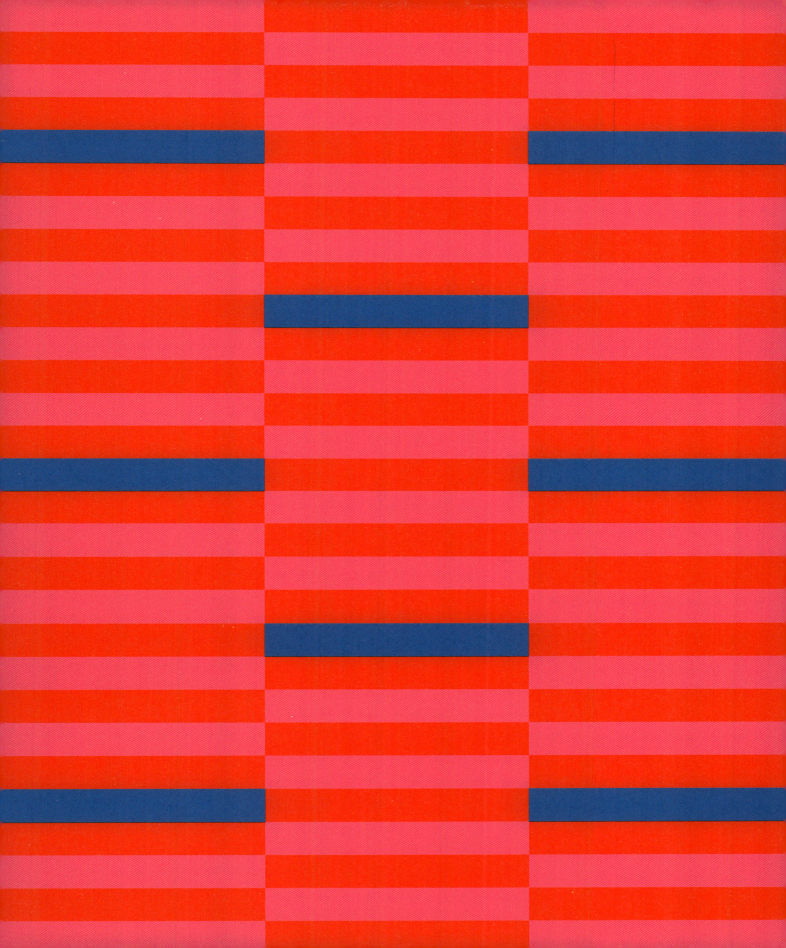

PINK LIKE RED BUT NOT QUITE

COLOUR COMBINATIONS

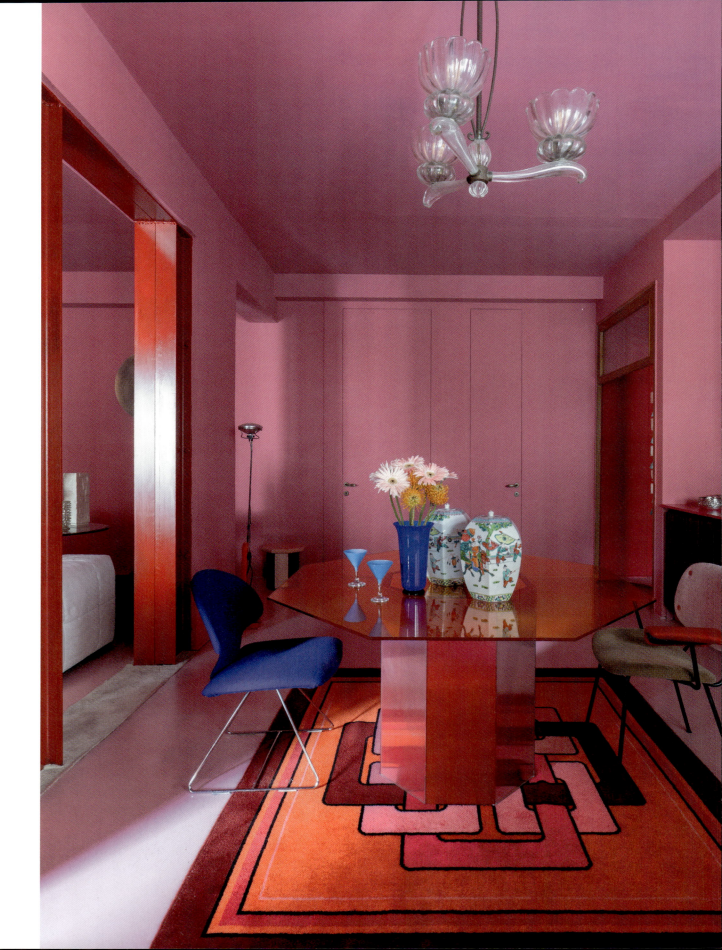

PINK LIKE RED BUT NOT QUITE

In 2023 designer Mariavittoria Paggini launched her most ambitious project: Casa Ornella – a multifaceted space located in Arezzo, Tuscany. It serves as a home, studio, showroom, and gallery, a melting pot of vibrant ideas, constantly changing to reflect Mariavittoria's preferences.

A bold and refined colour palette – characterised by contrasts and harmonies – is a signature element of Casa Ornella. While pink and red predominate the living area, the bedrooms feature deeper hues, such as violet and burgundy in her sons' rooms, while caramel and bright red tones grace the bathroom walls and floor. In the spare room, a mix of fuchsia and deep purple with a teal bedspread creates an ornate, sophisticated look.

(More about this particular colour combination on pages 120–125.) In her bedroom, shades of blush reappear, while the floor radiates vibrant fuchsia, and the walls are a shade of velvety black.

Many people might assume that painting a room pink and red will create a year-round Valentine's Day vibe (which is, come to think of it, not that bad). The pairing is certainly daring, but rules are made to be broken. Mariavittoria created a cohesive and contemporary space by using colour drenching – painting the walls, woodwork, ceiling, and doors in the same rich colour – adding an octagonal, translucent orange table and pops of blue. She cleverly chose a lighter shade of pink for the flooring, to avoid the feeling of being locked up in a heart-shaped chocolate box. Try shades with a pink undertone for rooms that have a lot of natural light. For a more dramatic, darker feel, try ones with red and purple undertones to create a luxurious atmosphere (also see pages 128-132).

104

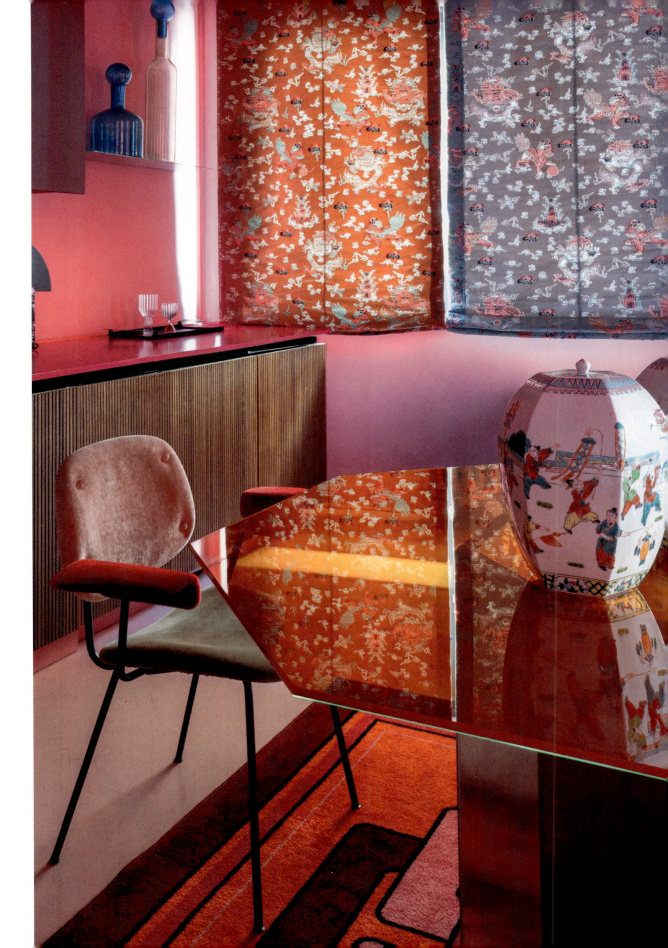

PINK LIKE RED BUT NOT QUITE

COLOUR COMBINATIONS

PINK LIKE RED BUT NOT QUITE

COLOUR COMBINATIONS

Mariavittoria bravely painted the walls of her bedroom black and paired them with a vibrant fuchsia floor. A simple gesture with a sumptuous result. On top of that, the contrast between lighter objects against the dark background emphasises finer details you might otherwise miss in a light-filled space. The caramel colour of the adjoining walk-in closet is a neutral packed with character that pretty much works alongside all other shades. It envelops and comforts, also making it a good shade in north-facing spaces or living areas. Here, caramel is combined with dark furniture and brass fixtures that contrast strikingly against the glossy red lacquer flooring, illuminated by a black-and-white vintage lamp.

The velvety black walls make for the perfect backdrop for Mariavittoria's vintage clothing – a cherished passion of hers.

PINK LIKE RED BUT NOT QUITE

COLOUR COMBINATIONS

COLOUR AS AN ACT OF HAPPINESS   COLOUR COMBINATIONS

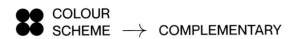

COLOUR SCHEME → **COMPLEMENTARY**

People immediately think of Barbie or flamingos when they hear pink. The colour is often even banished to the bedroom, as if it is some sort of secret guilty pleasure. But there are gorgeous, grounded, and modern shades of pink, even beautiful mid-toned pinks that are almost sand coloured, super sophisticated and far from gaudy or sugary.

COLOUR AS AN ACT OF HAPPINESS

When Tiphaine Verdier and her two children moved into the bourgeois Parisian building adjacent to Parc Monceau, she decided to add loads of personality to the space with vibrant, cheerful hues, transforming it into a cocoon of happiness without the fuss of renovating.

The apartment was – as J.R.R. Tolkien would call it – a glorious blank page, offering in many ways a fresh start. White and undeniably sterile, it presented limitations for its renters, as renovations were restricted and any decorative changes needed to be reversible. After years in London, Tiphaine blended her passion for interior design and vintage finds with inspiration drawn from British décor. Her home features a gorgeous collection of bold colours and collected pieces. The living room, for instance, exudes a cheerful and serene atmosphere with its mix of shrimp pink, warm caramel, and lemon yellow – a contemporary touch. As for the kitchen, it showcases a pinkish cherry red paired with a vibrant, pistachio green - reminiscent of traditional British green. Meanwhile, the dining room is adorned with a palette of softer mossy greens, evoking a cosy, countryside ambience. The chintz upholstery and floral artworks add an undeniably British charm to the space.

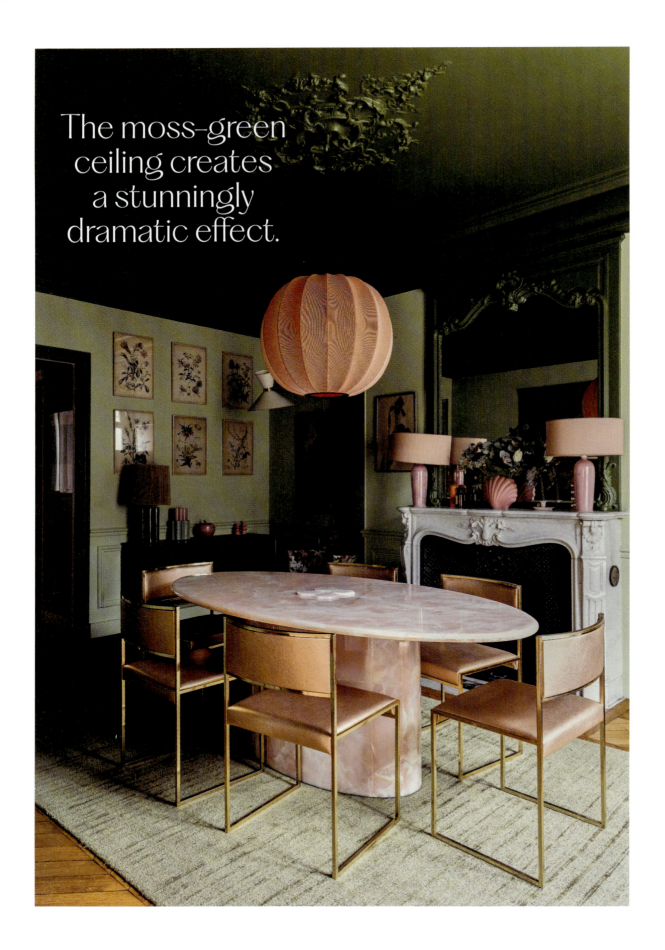

> The moss-green ceiling creates a stunningly dramatic effect.

COLOUR AS AN ACT OF HAPPINESS

COLOUR COMBINATIONS

COLOUR AS AN ACT OF HAPPINESS

COLOUR COMBINATIONS

Green is an incredibly versatile colour that suits most rooms. With so many shades of green available – some vastly different from others – it's essential to choose combinations thoughtfully. A helpful guideline is to stick to either yellow-based (commonly called olive, khaki, chartreuse, lime, pistachio, etc.) or blue-based greens (often with names like forest, emerald, bottle green, seafoam, etc.), as mixing the two can result in a jarring colour scheme. Rich, deep tones bring warmth to a space, making bold shades ideal for creating a cosy, cocoon-like atmosphere in north-facing rooms. In contrast, cooler green tones are better suited for the warmth of south-facing spaces. The charm of shrimp pink (or terracotta as an alternative – more about pink tones on pages 154–161) in the living room lies in its ability to create a warm, cocooning atmosphere without being overly sweet. As a warm mid-tone, it is especially suited for smaller rooms or spaces that lack (a lot of) natural light, as it helps hide shadows and adds depth. As mentioned earlier (pages 32–39), a single-coloured wall creates a strong contrast. By painting the entire room in a warm mid-tone, this contrast softens, resulting in a much subtler effect. Essentially, you're creating a canvas that still allows for bold splashes of colour in complementary tones (as Tiphaine did with the lemon couch), but analogous colour schemes are equally striking.

COLOUR COMBINATIONS   A COLOURFUL ODE TO MAX CLENDINNING

COLOUR SCHEME → SPLIT-COMPLEMENTARY

Teal is so versatile it seamlessly blends the tranquillity of blue with the richness of green. Like a tranquil day at the ocean on a beach lined with palm trees. This hybrid embodies the spirit of both sea and sky, radiating serenity with a dash of mystery. Many different shades can be produced from teal (or blue-green), from dark to light, from more green to more blue.

A COLOURFUL ODE TO MAX CLENDINNING

COLOUR COMBINATIONS

A COLOURFUL ODE TO MAX CLENDINNING

Housed within a sober and elegant building with balconies and large windows, this 200-square-metre Milan apartment was a time capsule left untouched for 10 years and required extensive renovation. Today it is a striking surprise of colour, carefully curated by architect and interior decorator Patricia Bohrer.

Patricia's interior design is a dedicated homage to the visionary Max Clendinning, a British architect, interior designer, sculptor, and artist who eschewed minimalism. Bold combinations and warm, bright tones dominate the living area, while softer hues create a tranquil ambience in the private rooms. The living room highlights include the vibrant reinterpretation of a timeless classic, Rietveld's Utrecht armchairs paired with Pierre Frey's colourful velvet curtains and cyan Chinese Art Deco carpet. Complementing these pieces is a collection of bespoke furnishings crafted by Patricia, such as the wall-mounted bookcase in the living room.

Patricia created a highly personal modern kaleidoscope of design expressed through various volumes and textures across fabrics, wallpapers, and bespoke furniture like the pleated console next to the dining table. It all reflects her mixed Spanish and Hungarian heritage and her deep admiration for the aesthetics of the 1960s and 1970s.

A COLOURFUL ODE TO MAX CLENDINNING

COLOUR COMBINATIONS

A COLOURFUL ODE TO MAX CLENDINNING

COLOUR COMBINATIONS

Teal green, yellow, red, pink, and violet sit opposite each other on the colour wheel, making them complementary colours. Rich jewel tones add a satisfying contrast to teal; together they create a luxurious and opulent feel. In the dining space, teal's calming presence harmonises beautifully with the vibrant energy of the warm side of the spectrum. Together, they forge a mid-century atmosphere that sparks a sense of joy with loads of gorgeous contrast to boot.

    Sunlit rooms pair particularly well with teal; it tempers intense sunlight while maintaining an invigorating ambience. But can teal really do no wrong? You might wonder. It does have one potential drawback: in small spaces, teal can feel oppressive. You can counteract this effect by incorporating metallic accents or, as Patricia wisely did, introducing white into adjacent areas. In this case, the living room features a warm palette of purples, oranges, shades of fuchsia, and cyan set against crisp white walls. In a book about colour, it might seem strange to advocate for white walls, but as you can see in Patricia's home, white walls provide a canvas that allows endless variation with colour. This combination not only makes the vibrant hues pop but also visually expands the teal-accented dining space, creating a seamless and inviting transition.

HOMAGE TO THE RED LILY OF FLORENCE • COLOUR COMBINATIONS

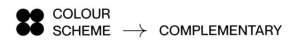
COLOUR SCHEME → COMPLEMENTARY

Red is the first colour that humans mastered, fabricated, reproduced, and broke down into different shades. It is also one of the earliest colours used by artists during the prehistoric period. As a deep shade of red, burgundy embodies the passionate energy of red, yet with a refined and dignified demeanour. It is solid and traditional without being stodgy.

HOMAGE TO THE RED LILY OF FLORENCE

In homage to the red lily of Florence, designer Valentina Guidi Ottobri drenched the 37-square-metre dwelling in the Sant'Ambrogio district in Florence in red. Her vision for the interior was simple yet ingenious: it had to feel like a 'postcard from Florence' – an interior inspired by the Florentine Renaissance and its ideals, such as the rediscovery of nature and the study of classical masterpieces.

HOMAGE TO THE RED LILY OF FLORENCE

COLOUR COMBINATIONS

HOMAGE TO THE RED LILY OF FLORENCE

COLOUR COMBINATIONS

> The light blue of the beams echoes the sky on the fresco depicting a unicorn by artist Marco Pace.

This meant restoring the plaster-boarded beams to their original beauty and incorporating aesthetics rooted in Florentine traditions. Terracotta elements, like the washbasin and plant pots, pay tribute to the historic kilns of Impruneta – a town near Florence. The accompanying palette celebrates the colours of fruits the 15th century Medici collected and grew in large Impruneta pots, like lemons, oranges, and bergamot.

If you're not that much into Moulin Rouge core, raw materials like uneven Moroccan tiles (called zellige), untreated wood, and rough beams add texture and contrast to the deep reds, preventing the feeling that you step into a nightclub (unless that's what you're after, of course). In the bedroom, open-weave throw pillows, rattan bedside tables, and headboards enhance the rustic charm of the Florentine-inspired design.

How we perceive colour is subjective and influenced by the surrounding colours and textures. It is sometimes still hard to see the subtle variations on small paint swatches. Instead of painting the test colour directly on a wall, paint it on a large piece of cardboard so you can move it around. This way, you can evaluate the colour in different rooms and under changing light conditions. By testing colours alongside the floor, you can see how they appear in your specific space and avoid disappointing results.

When working with an analogous colour scheme featuring shades like marsala, maroon, burgundy, eggplant, and wine, it's helpful to distinguish between them, as they can appear similar until applied, such as on walls. Wine is lighter and more red; eggplant is a dark, brownish purple (like the Moroccan kitchen tiles); burgundy is a deep red with a purple undertone, maroon – derived from the French word marron meaning chestnut – is a mix of red and brown; marsala is dusky and faded with brown undertones, here paired beautifully with the tiles. As shown in Valentina's interior, these reds and red-adjacent tones pair harmoniously with peach, blush, taupes, greys, ochres, dark browns, pinks, golden yellows, but also turquoise and teal.

HOMAGE TO THE RED LILY OF FLORENCE

COLOUR COMBINATIONS

COLOUR COMBINATIONS   NOSTALGIC COLOURS, CLASHING PATTERNS

COLOUR SCHEME → SPLIT-COMPLEMENTARY

Retro colour palettes provide a delightful nod to the past, adding a touch of nostalgia and personality to modern interiors or, in this case, a former factory. These often bold and sometimes quite unexpected combinations can rejuvenate a space, adding personality and the warmth and charm of mid-century design and other timeless styles.

NOSTALGIC COLOURS, CLASHING PATTERNS

A stone's throw away from the vibrant centre of Milan, tucked away at the end of a small street, you'll find the home and workshop of interior designer Stefania Passera. The 200-square-metre space, with its industrial character – for it was a former elevator factory – demonstrates how styles, colours, and shapes can be combined to create a unique and creative signature.

Stefania's philosophy of life is to follow her imagination and make bold interior choices, like the colourful chairs on the yellow-green carpet, the wall decoration behind the dining table, and the lemon-patterned wallpaper in the bathroom. The collection of furniture is carefully curated; according to Stefania they represent freedom and creativity. And she wants everybody who visits to experience that feeling.

The mid-century furniture and wall panelling, both featuring clear, clean lines, provide the perfect pared-back backdrop for more romantic accessories like the intricate mirror frame and dusty pink lampion.

By incorporating floral motifs, grasscloth wallpaper, and a mid-century palette of earthy tones such as avocado green, soft browns, dusty pinks, and subtle hints of teal, the design evokes the charm of past decades while also proving that different styles from different eras can be perfectly blended into a unique, curated whole.

On page 117, I stated that it's generally best to avoid mixing greens with yellow and blue undertones. However, the beauty of playing with colour is that it's a bit like the pirate's code – more of a guideline than a strict set of rules. Stefania, who often replaces furniture, proves that mixing yellow and blue undertones can work. While the rug has an overall distinct yellow undertone – almost leaning towards lime – the green cabinets are a much cooler shade.

That rug is the key: look closer and you'll see how beautifully it pulls the space together. Its pattern's varied shades of green and brown complement the wooden chairs, coffee table, and the cabinets, thereby creating that harmony. Notice, too, how the cool blues in the pattern on the chairs echo the blue tones of the Indian daybed, adding another layer of cohesion to the design. In essence, if you're looking to adjust your colour palette, ensure there are key objects that reflect the chosen palette.

The kitchen is an excellent space to explore retro colour schemes. The contemporary cabinetry in harvest yellow, combined with vintage and even romantic designs, creates a functional yet nostalgic space.

138

NOSTALGIC COLOURS, CLASHING PATTERNS

COLOUR COMBINATIONS

REFLECTIONS OF MOUNT VESUVIUS AND THE SEA   COLOUR COMBINATIONS

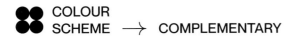

COLOUR SCHEME → COMPLEMENTARY

Blue is the coolest colour on the colour wheel, yet it elicits warm days in countless ways. Think of the sea, a cloudless sky, or the swimming pool. Just looking at a blue room can slow your pace and calm you down. And with its wide range of shades and tones – from the lively and dynamic turquoise to the rich and enigmatic navy blue offers incredible versatility in design.

REFLECTIONS OF MOUNT VESUVIUS AND THE SEA

The building dates back to a time marked by the construction of many prestigious projects that offered spacious apartments with panoramic views, nestled amidst the lush greenery of historic Naples gardens. The main challenge for architect Giuliano Andrea dell'Uva was to preserve the original 1960s character of the building while transforming it into a contemporary family home.

To achieve this, Giuliano incorporated floor tiles designed by Gio Ponti, still produced in Vietri near Naples, and combined design icons from the 1930s, 1960s, and 1970s. Additionally, he used a variety of materials and colours to give each space a distinct identity. Richly pigmented colours like green, blue, and marigold were chosen to create unique geometric patterns, reflecting the surrounding colours of the sky, sea, and greenery. The result is a harmonious interplay of contemporary design, nostalgic elements, and traditional influences, beautifully reflecting the preferences and lifestyle of owner Maria Fiore and her family.

REFLECTIONS OF MOUNT VESUVIUS AND THE SEA

COLOUR COMBINATIONS

REFLECTIONS OF MOUNT VESUVIUS AND THE SEA

COLOUR COMBINATIONS

The use of wood brings warmth and tranquillity to the blue palette in the kitchen.

Dark wooden finishes throughout the apartment lend the interior an understated richness and warmth, giving off an almost Zen-like tranquillity. The bedroom is painted in a rich emerald green, making the space feel like a cocoon. The dramatic palette enhances the interplay of daylight reflecting off the Japanese screen – mounted on the wall as a piece of art – and the polished brass vintage chandelier. The result is stunningly opulent.

The use of predominantly dark colours in interior design arouses extreme emotions. Advocates appreciate their elegance and dramatic impact, while others worry that darker tones might give the feeling of being trapped in a black hole. Shades such as black and deep navy add sophistication, luxury, depth, and character to an interior. However, it's also important to consider their potential drawbacks. Dark colours can visually shrink a room, making them less ideal for small spaces. They also require carefully planned, often stronger lighting to prevent the room from feeling heavy or gloomy. Additionally, dark surfaces tend to highlight scratches, dust, and dirt more easily, making them higher maintenance. If you're sensitive to either or both, it may be wise to opt for a lighter alternative, such as a monochrome palette of black and white or (dark) grey and off-white.

Overall, the rich, moody colour palette is broken up with light accents in the form of accessories, mirrors, shiny surfaces, greenery, and, for example, the marigold rounded sofa. Even the big blue rug seems to be reflecting light. Black and deep navy work very well with jewel colours, but pairing them with a soft tone like the blue-green wall in the sitting room softens the contrast.

COLOUR COMBINATIONS	RIDING A PINK CLOUD

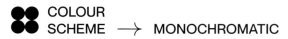

COLOUR SCHEME → MONOCHROMATIC

From the earthy pink limewash of 16th-century manor houses to the rosy hues of Edwardian dining rooms, the love for pink predates Barbie's Malibu dreamhouse by centuries. Pantone's selection of rose quartz – a dusty, almost muddied shade – as one of its colours of the year in 2016 reignited our pink obsession, giving rise to the phenomenon now known as Millennial Pink or Tumblr pink.

RIDING A PINK CLOUD

The Musée Yves Saint Laurent in Marrakech was one of the inspirations for the blush pink Clarens building, designed by Malcolm Kluk and Christiaan Gabriël du Toit. The soft pink façade softens the harsh architectural lines, while the interior and exterior of the building are designed to work in harmony – enveloping its inhabitants in nature.

> Black suspended ceiling rails on a white ceiling create a modern graphic effect.

The four-storey building, containing several condo-style units, is located in Fresnaye, Cape Town, and blends the retro allure of Palm Springs modernism with the atmosphere of apartment living as portrayed in the 1990s TV series Melrose Place. The interior design serves as a hub of inspiration and experimentation for Malcolm and Christiaan. It showcases a curated collection of bold pieces accumulated over the years, often repurposed, reupholstered, or resprayed to align with their evolving vision. The blush pink curved wall – which looks so soft you want to stroke it – plays a central role in the design, seamlessly matching the exterior brickwork to enhance the indoor-outdoor connection. The blush pink is balanced by the contrast of slate flooring, layered with soft grey carpeting and sculptural elements in leather and wood. Whoever said pink is just for kids' rooms will think again when they see this: the palette, paired with bold, edgy furniture, radiates sophistication, sexiness, and undeniable allure.

Using a single shade to fill a space can sometimes feel overwhelming. Finding balance, as Malcolm and Christiaan have done, is essential. It's important to prioritise what a room needs over what colour you want. Pink, for instance, is an incredibly versatile colour, but it can be tricky to get just right. The key lies in understanding its undertones (see page 9), which generally fall into three main categories. First, there are pinks with brown undertones. These are the most stable pinks, reacting minimally to changes in light or exposure to cooler light, which might alter other shades. Second, there are pinks with peach undertones that are warm and inviting – these pinks often carry a very subtle peachy hue, creating a classic sugary pink – the quintessential definition of pink. And then there are pinks with grey undertones. These are the coolest and often the most sophisticated shades. However, lighting is crucial when using them. In dimly lit, north-facing rooms, they can appear lavender or even verge on mauve. The secret to working with pink lies in the lighting, so test colours thoroughly and compare them before applying them to the walls. (Read about testing colours on page 128-132.)

RIDING A PINK CLOUD

COLOUR COMBINATIONS

EXPRESS YOURSELF/DON'T REPRESS YOURSELF — COLOUR COMBINATIONS

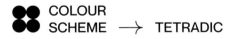

COLOUR SCHEME → **TETRADIC**

While ochre is often associated with a golden yellow hue, its colour can range from yellow to reddish and brownish, depending on the elements present in the earth. In some cases, it can even exhibit subtle violet or bluish tones. This versatile hue has been used since prehistoric times, making it one of the oldest pigments known to humanity.

EXPRESS YOURSELF/ DON'T REPRESS YOURSELF

Housed in a Haussmannian building in the heart of Lyon's charming district of antique dealers, galleries, and décor boutiques, Claude Cartier's apartment is a living embodiment of her interior design and colour visions.

Over her 40-year career as an interior designer, Claude has never been one to follow convention. Renowned for pushing boundaries and embracing the unexpected, her eponymous studio has built a reputation for its eclectic and daring style. For her latest project, her own home, the challenge was to create a bold and joyous colour palette that truly reflected her personality and her deep love for the Mediterranean colour palette of kiln-baked earthiness. Claude's fearless approach and her signature use of rich, sumptuous tones juxtaposed with light, uplifting hues reach new heights in her 120-square-metre apartment-cum-showroom in Lyon. Reinvented every six months, it serves as a dynamic canvas for Claude's evolving creativity, always offering a fresh perspective.

EXPRESS YOURSELF/DON'T REPRESS YOURSELF

COLOUR COMBINATIONS

EXPRESS YOURSELF/DON'T REPRESS YOURSELF

COLOUR COMBINATIONS

The entrance of the apartment immediately showcases the audacious colour palette that runs throughout the space. Dramatic tones like burnt saffron and black trimmings create a beautiful contrast against the black-and-white chequerboard flooring, while mint-green pastels and watery shades of pearly whites, dove greys and pinks bring a fresh, airy vibe – also showing how to go bold with pale colours. These elements are further enlivened by dots of saturated colours like turquoise and purple (and even some unexpected red in the flower shaped throw pillow). The overall design is further packed with personality in the shape of deliciously playful Memphis Milano-inspired patterns.

Overall, Claude's apartment is a joyful environment that buzzes with colour and pattern, a cohesive interplay of shapes and hues that shifts focus from one room to the next. This succession of room sets has another advantage – it gives the impression of a bigger space. Claude shows that by skilfully incorporating textures and patterns, one doesn't have to rely solely on paint to transform a space. The arch in the ceiling between the hallway and living room is mirrored in the arrangement of black-and-white tiles on the floor below. Meanwhile, the postmodern-shaped rug subtly reflects the hallway's colour palette. Textiles offer another clever way to introduce colour and have the added benefit of being easily changeable. Curtains play a subtle yet effective role in defining the living area, with Claude choosing aquamarine velour drapes that span an entire wall. These can be drawn back to reveal her book collection, adding both functionality and... more colour!

EXPRESS YOURSELF/DON'T REPRESS YOURSELF

COLOUR COMBINATIONS

EXPRESS YOURSELF/DON'T REPRESS YOURSELF

COLOUR COMBINATIONS

COLOUR COMBINATIONS   A WHITE CANVAS PACKED WITH PLAYFULNESS

COLOUR SCHEME → SPLIT-COMPLEMENTARY

White is the least offensive colour in the spectrum. It doesn't bother, doesn't clash, and in these colour-drenched times, it is almost considered conventional, dull, and colourless both literally and figuratively. However, in its purest form, white represents peace and fresh beginnings, and as the primary colour in interior design, its versatility and adaptability allow for easy adjustments to secondary and accent colours.

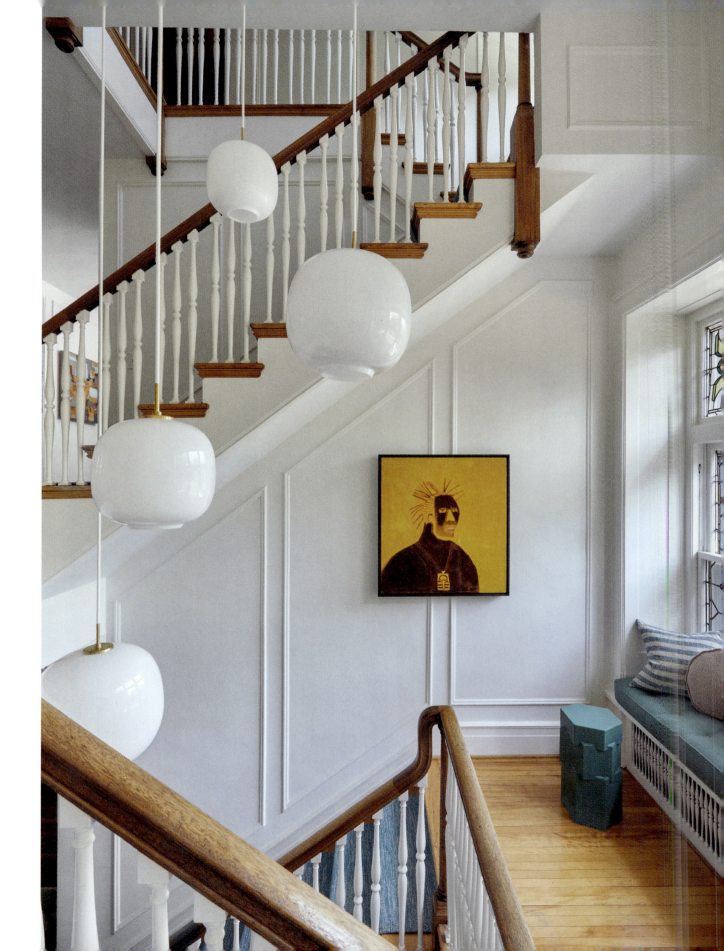

A WHITE CANVAS PACKED WITH PLAYFULNESS

COLOUR COMBINATIONS

A WHITE CANVAS PACKED WITH PLAYFULNESS

This grand 1920s Edwardian-style shingle house in Pelham, New York, is perched high above a sloping garden, offering sweeping views over the treetops of the surrounding landscape. It feels a world apart from the hustle and bustle of New York City, just 20 miles away.

After housing multiple generations of residents – and even serving as the consulate for Barbados at one point – the house had already been meticulously restored by its previous owner. However, when Erica and Andrew Holborn purchased it, they felt it needed a touch more schwung – a modern perspective and some youthful energy. Interior designers Gregory Dufner and Daniel Heighes Wismer were tasked with embracing the building's prestigious architectural heritage and abundance of natural light, while also finding a careful balance between pushing boundaries and knowing exactly when to exercise restraint.

Gregory and Daniel introduced colourful, contemporary furniture, wall coverings, fabrics, and artwork, perfectly suited to the dynamic needs of a young, growing family. The dining room in particular serves as the home's centrepiece, featuring a bold, graphic wall covering that extends seamlessly across the ceiling above the existing

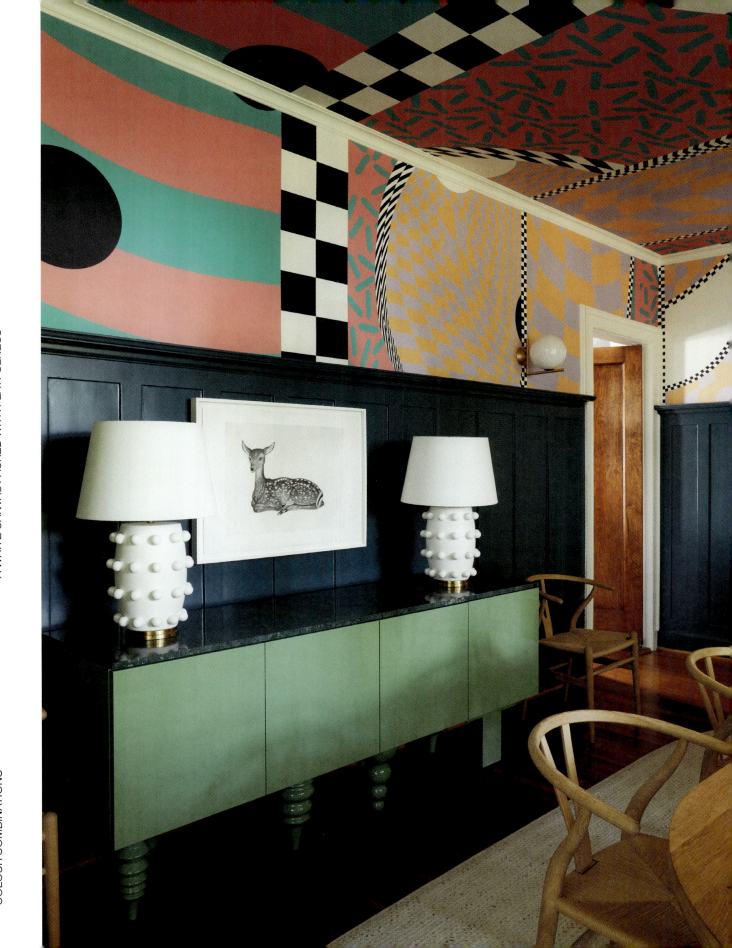

A WHITE CANVAS PACKED WITH PLAYFULNESS

COLOUR COMBINATIONS

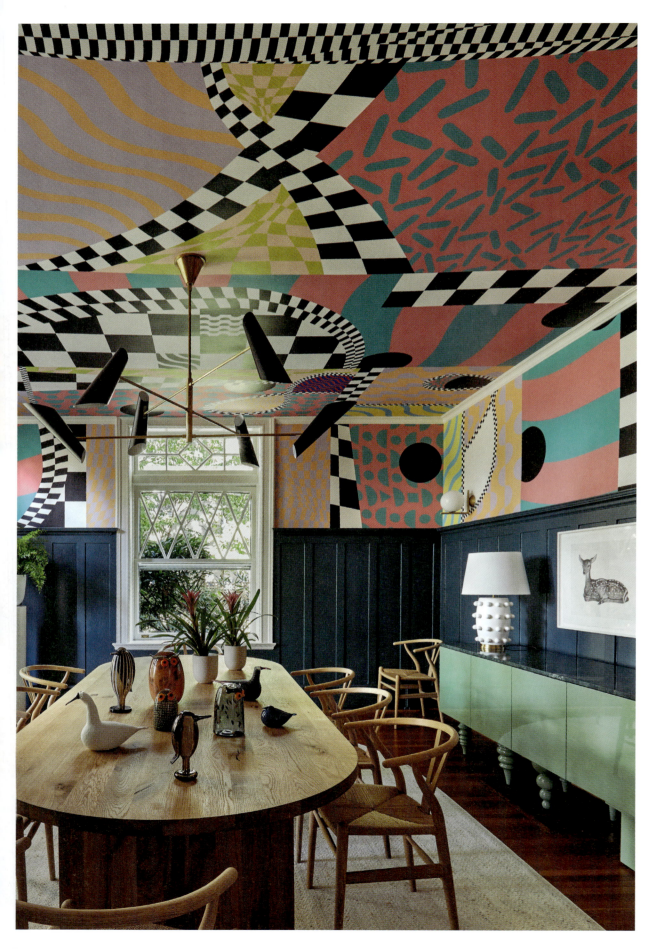

A WHITE CANVAS PACKED WITH PLAYFULNESS

COLOUR COMBINATIONS

> Rounded shapes softly contrast with the clean, white walls, while naturally warm wood adds a touch of cosiness.

panelling. The original panels received a beautiful petrol green colour that blends sublimely with the playful wallpaper above.

To honour the client's desire for simplicity in the traditional elements, the designers painted all the walls white and preserved much of the natural oak panelling. However, a neutral base like that doesn't have to be as uninspiring as it might sound. To prevent a home from feeling like a bland bowl of yogurt, you use that white canvas to your advantage – as a foundation on which to pack loads of character and colour. Keep in mind that white isn't simply white, though. There are dozens of different shades of white paint that, if used incorrectly, can wreak havoc on the aesthetic of a space. The perfect white paint colour might look great in your dining room when it's empty, think about what the space will look like when it is full. The colour of surrounding woods, fabrics, and soft furnishings can reflect off the white, subtly altering its shade, as can the room's orientation and the amount of natural light it receives. Also, be mindful of undertones. In heritage homes with added character, opt for whites with subtle yellow or beige undertones. These shades complement period features and textural, natural materials like timber beautifully. In essence, treat your choice of white the same way you would a shade of pistachio green, fuchsia, or butter yellow. Start by testing the hue in the space with a (large) paint swatch to see how it interacts with the room.

> The dove white cabinets subtly downplay the classical detailing, lending the space a more modern vibe.

A WHITE CANVAS PACKED WITH PLAYFULNESS

COLOUR COMBINATIONS

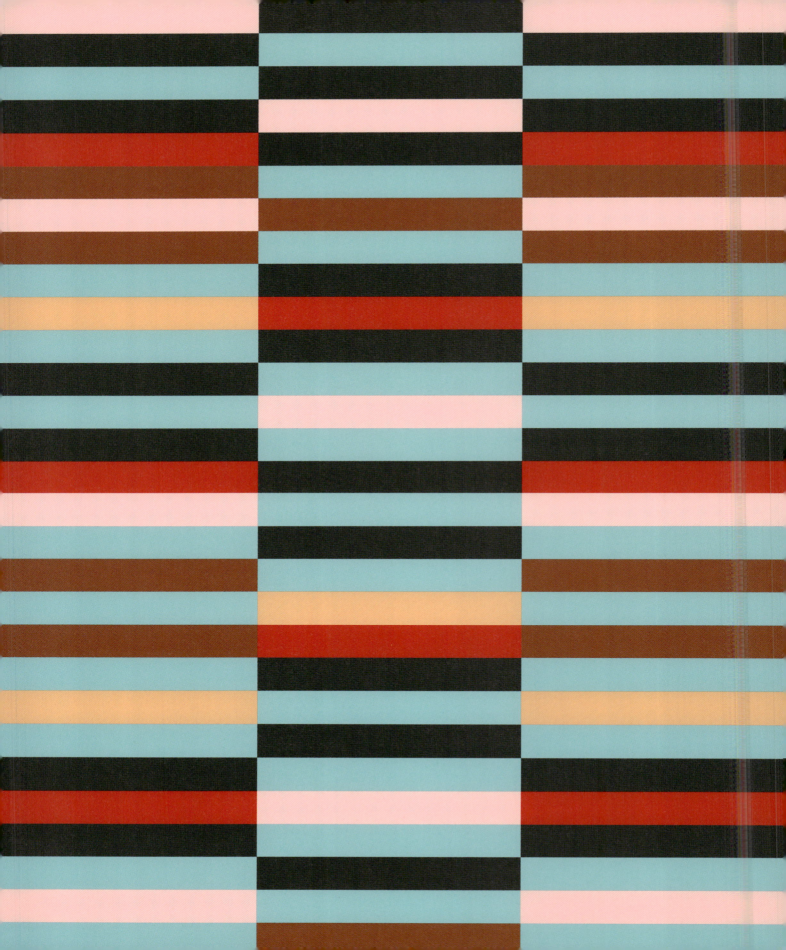

UNCONVENTIONAL ROOM WITH A VIEW   COLOUR COMBINATIONS

COLOUR
SCHEME → SPLIT-COMPLEMENTARY

Green, whether in the form of plants or accent walls, gives a space a natural element, softening and enhancing the overall visual appeal of a space. From ferns to succulents and every variety in between, nature's beauty has the power to transform a house into a home. Available in a variety of shades, houseplants serve as statement pieces, adding depth, texture, and colour to your interior design, much like soft furnishings and decorative accessories.

UNCONVENTIONAL ROOM WITH A VIEW

Fashion designer Isabela Capeto has always dreamed of living with a view of Rio de Janeiro's iconic Sugarloaf Mountain. Today, she enjoys this postcard-perfect scene every day from her 270-square-metre urban jungle.

Isabela hired architect Beto Figueiredo to oversee the structural renovations and redesign the floor plan, creating a more open and cohesive layout. Naturally, the overall interior design is her own creation.

What makes Isabela's home truly unique is her ability to seamlessly blend the traditional elements of the original 1940s architecture – such as crown mouldings, high ceilings, and parquet floors in two shades of wood – with the warm, inviting mix of prints that earned her fame as a designer. It's a beautiful fusion of European architectural adornments and the distinctly Brazilian style that defines her designs. During her travels around the world, Isabela fills her suitcases with a variety of fabrics, which she seamlessly mixes and matches to her interior design upon returning home. The abundance of houseplants connects the interior with the building's exterior, strengthening the connection to the lush, verdant outdoors.

When you first glance at Isabela's interior, it might appear as though everything has been randomly put together. But nothing could be further from the truth. Because the turquoise and brown are reflected in the leaves of the different kind of plants and the flooring and furniture, but in different shades, it still creates a cohesive look – maintaining a certain optical calmness despite the rich patterns, textures, found treasures, and added accent colours.

UNCONVENTIONAL ROOM WITH A VIEW

COLOUR COMBINATIONS

The kitchen is a wonderful, colourful mix of pots, bowls, fruit, flowers, and works of art.

The whole may seem busy, but if you look closely, you'll see that Isabela consistently uses a palette of reds (from red to brown), greens, and blues (from turquoise to a richly saturated blue) on a white canvas. This allows her to really experiment with textures, patterns, objects, and found treasures while still keeping it cohesive. Her tactile ceramic wall objects serve as delightful accents on the wall, like cherries on a delicious, richly decorated cake. Isabela created eye-catching accents by painting certain door styles and passages turquoise. For those hesitant to embrace vivid hues, this approach provides a manageable way to add bold colours without feeling overwhelmed (see also page 204-211).

Working with greens and blues arouses the feeling of calm because they tend to symbolise the natural world. Reminiscent of endless tropical skies and oceans, the greens and turquoise elements combined with crisp white walls bring a refreshing vitality to Isabela's interior – even on the gloomiest days.

COLOUR COMBINATIONS   CURIOUS AND CURIOUSER

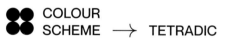

COLOUR SCHEME → TETRADIC

The combination of green and pink is a timeless classic. They go together like Glinda and Elphaba. The reason why they pair so beautifully is their contrasting yet complementary qualities – pink's vibrancy is tempered by green's refreshing tone. Just imagine a lush green garden adorned with bright pink flowers – it's a perfect harmony of nature's palette.

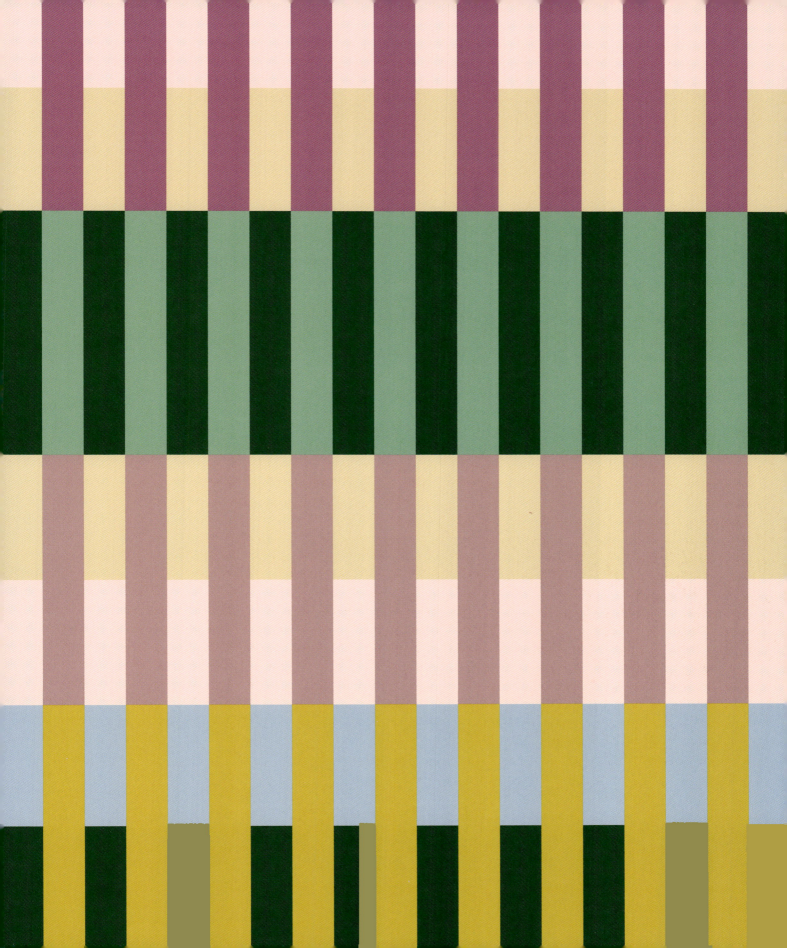

CURIOUS AND CURIOUSER

This house is a fusion of Georgian and mid-century architecture – a blend that immediately captivated interior designer Joanne Burgess. Her challenge was to honour both eras, creating a cosy, vibrant family home while preserving the building's distinctive charm and character.

The house – a Grade II listed Georgian property in Henley, which began life as a coaching inn – is rumoured to have hosted the King of Denmark. Over the years, it took on various identities, serving as a finishing school, an architect's office, a shop, and, more recently, a bed and breakfast. Each chapter in its history brought unique additions, including a curved wooden staircase in the sitting room and a suspended ceiling, hanging just inches below the floor above. Today, the house is a fusion of Georgian and mid-century architecture – a blend that immediately captivated interior designer Joanne Burgess. Her challenge was to honour both eras, creating a cosy, vibrant family home while preserving the building's distinctive charm and character. Joanne, known for her expertise in blending diverse styles, embraced the challenge of crafting eclectic spaces where every room tells its own story. To achieve this vision, she flawlessly incorporated mid-century design elements and materials, with beech plywood featured prominently throughout the home. She paired these with influences from the bold, playful aesthetic of the Italian postmodernist Memphis Milano movement. A curated mix of second-hand furniture and accessories adds a contemporary, dynamic touch, ensuring the interiors remain fresh, stylish, and full of personality. Fun fact: Joanne sticks to themes when it comes to artworks – food-related in the kitchen and, for example, ships in the bathroom. The walls and stairs are adorned with a palette of blues, greens, and pinks, seamlessly connecting the newer sections of the house with the meticulously preserved Georgian features. Joanne's take on green is fresh and light, the overall bucolic palette and patterned wallpapers creating a feeling of a contemporary fable.

Another feature that immediately catches the eye is the statement wallpapered walls. Before diving into specific wallpaper patterns, consider the overall space you're designing and the mood you want to create. If you're aiming for a soothing atmosphere, you may want to rethink that bold, busy pattern you've been eyeing. The size of a room also influences the scale of the print you should choose. A very large print may overwhelm a small wall, while a smaller print might get lost on a larger wall. If you're adding wallpaper to an existing room, rather than starting from scratch, consider the colours already present in the space, such as those in the furniture, window treatments, and flooring. Choose a wallpaper that either complements or thoughtfully contrasts these hues – colour theory can be a helpful guide here. For surrounding walls, consider selecting a colour found in the wallpaper.

Maximalist and daring, the hallway is the perfect example of pattern drenching.

CURIOUS AND CURIOUSER

COLOUR COMBINATIONS

A MARRIAGE BETWEEN VIBRANCY AND SUBTLETY COLOUR COMBINATIONS

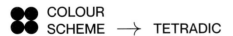
COLOUR SCHEME → TETRADIC

COLOUR THEORY

The pastel aesthetic is far from new – soft, sugary tones have been cherished since the 18th century, especially in the lavishly adorned Rococo interiors. However, these gentle hues are experiencing a modern revival, and in this new chapter of interior design, a captivating trend is taking centre stage: the impeccable fusion of bold and pastel colours – a truly divine marriage of vibrancy and subtlety.

A MARRIAGE BETWEEN VIBRANCY AND SUBTLETY

The charming 1920s villa is located in the heart of a small town in the Luberon region, France, surrounded by picturesque countryside and just a 20-minute drive from Aix-en-Provence. The two-storey 130-square-metre house, with its façade in warm earth tones, white-framed windows, and sage green shutters, is the quintessential Provençal home.

After being abandoned for about two decades, the house was in a state of disrepair, with a leaky roof and a garden that had become an overgrown jungle. However, the lengthy to-do list didn't faze decorator and colour expert Marine Koprivnjak and artist-craftsman Victor Chabaud. To transform the house into the headquarters of their creative endeavours, they revised the original layout, removed some partitions, and converted the old kitchen into their study. From the outside, the house appears to be in its original state. Upon entering, you are immersed in a vibrant kaleidoscope of colour. The first thing to catch your eye is how colour defines and decorates the space. Marine masterfully used colour to punctuate clean lines and bold geometric shapes, drawing inspiration from legendary architects like Barragán and Bofill.

A MARRIAGE BETWEEN VIBRANCY AND SUBTLETY

COLOUR COMBINATIONS

Shades of green, yellow, burgundy, blue, brown, and lilac – interspersed with abundant pink – flow through the rooms, occasionally interrupted by neutral walls – to keep things from getting overwhelming. The palette of tones – a custom-made blend of natural pigments and plaster made by Victor – shifts subtly with the changing light throughout the day.

    Pastel colours are ideal for effortless colour combinations, as their pale grey or white undertones ensure they blend harmoniously. The softer and more neutral the tones, the more you can combine them together. The true magic, however, lies in the combination of bold, muted, and pastel colours. For example, the chocolate brown chair and dots of bright yellow, burgundy, and cobalt blue in the dusty beige built-in cabinet serve as a focal point, while pastel pink archways in the hallway add a touch of softness to the bold green space. For the study, Victor cleverly mixed a soft ethereal lilac with an earth pigment to avoid things becoming too sugary (more about undertones in pink hues on pages 154–161). By doing so, it combines beautifully with warm greys and off-white, but also with warmer tones like butter yellow, orange, khaki, and sage. In the bedroom, Marine and Victor blended earthy tones with accents of lilac and yellow. It crafts a distinctive cocoon that bridges the 1970s aesthetic with Provençal charm.

207

A MARRIAGE BETWEEN VIBRANCY AND SUBTLETY

COLOUR COMBINATIONS

A MARRIAGE BETWEEN VIBRANCY AND SUBTLETY

COLOUR COMBINATIONS

COLOUR COMBINATIONS   PRIMARY COLOURS UNDER THE EAVES

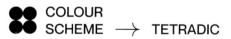

COLOUR SCHEME → **TETRADIC**

To introduce surprise and delight into an interior, consider using bold, vibrant hues to accentuate structural quirks like load-bearing columns or architectural features such as alcoves, niches, and built-in shelving. By highlighting these elements with striking colours, you can add character and depth, transforming often-overlooked features into eye-catching focal points.

PRIMARY COLOURS UNDER THE EAVES

COLOUR COMBINATIONS

PRIMARY COLOURS UNDER THE EAVES

After six months of renovations, the 78-square-metre former maid's quarters – known in Paris as a chambre de bonne – located on the top floor of a building in Neuilly-Plaisance, was transformed into the vibrant and family-friendly haven interior designer Nicolas Payet envisioned.

Painting the walls is undoubtedly one of the simplest yet most impactful ways to transform a home with a fresh look and mood. And when Nicolas purchased his attic apartment, it was in dire need of a makeover. Inspired by his childhood love of treehouses, he set out to create a contemporary and colourful cabin-like retreat. Colour is omnipresent, even embracing structural quirks like the unavoidable load-bearing column in the kitchen. Instead of hiding it with white paint, Nicolas turned it into an architectural feature, painting it emerald green – the unifying hue of the project.

There won't be many interior designers who would recommend buying furniture before moving into a new home, but love is a feeling that can't be stopped. That's how it happened that Nicolas had already purchased his emerald green sofa long before he had a house to put it in. The emerald green eventually became the starting point for the colour palette in the Payet household. Hints of this fresh tone

are now echoed in the arches Nicolas incorporated into the walls of the open-plan living area. It flows seamlessly along the skirting boards, is highlighted around door frames, and is even reflected in lighting and accessories.

Earlier, I discussed the advantages of using white tones to enhance an interior design (see pages 120-125). Nicolas effectively incorporated white to highlight his colour palette. The white trim along the kitchen counter, off-white kitchen door, and the arched alcoves in the living room serve as clean, crisp borders, beautifully accentuating the contrasting colours of adjacent areas. Using colour to divide a space also aids in defining its functions. In the bedroom/study, Nicolas combined white with a muted olive green, allowing the eye to easily interpret the room's layout. (See pages 22-29 for more on half-painted walls.) This technique of incorporating white into a design creates clear visual distinctions between spaces. When experimenting with white, consider testing different shades before application. Bright white lends a sleek, contemporary aesthetic, while softer, creamy whites add warmth to a room.

Beautifully contrasted against the beige walls and warm wooden flooring, the baby-blue cabinetry really stands out. The warm undertones of the neutral surfaces enhance and complement the blue, creating a harmonious balance.

PRIMARY COLOURS UNDER THE EAVES

COLOUR COMBINATIONS

PRIMARY COLOURS UNDER THE EAVES

COLOUR COMBINATIONS

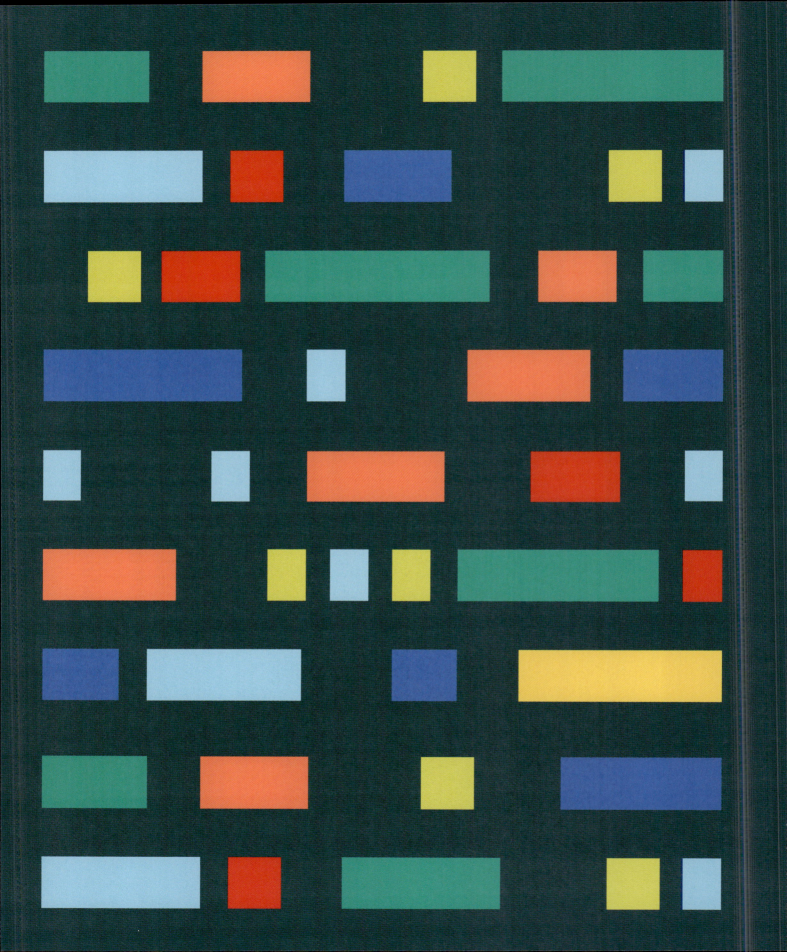

QUIRKY CURIOSITIES, MUTED COLOURS COLOUR COMBINATIONS

COLOUR SCHEME → SPLIT-COMPLEMENTARY

Every interior with a harmonious and visually balanced look is an interplay between muted and saturated colours. When every element of your interior features bold, bright colours, they all compete for attention at once. Pairing vibrant hues with muted tones enhances balance and allows bright colours to stand out or 'pop', helping you create distinct focal points.

QUIRKY CURIOSITIES, MUTED COLOURS

To create more space for their growing family, South African interior designer Sarah Ord and her husband, Nigel, moved from a small house in Cape Town's city centre to the family home where her mother had previously lived, nestled in the leafy suburb of Claremont. Colour – just one of Sarah's many interior fascinations – was an immediate priority.

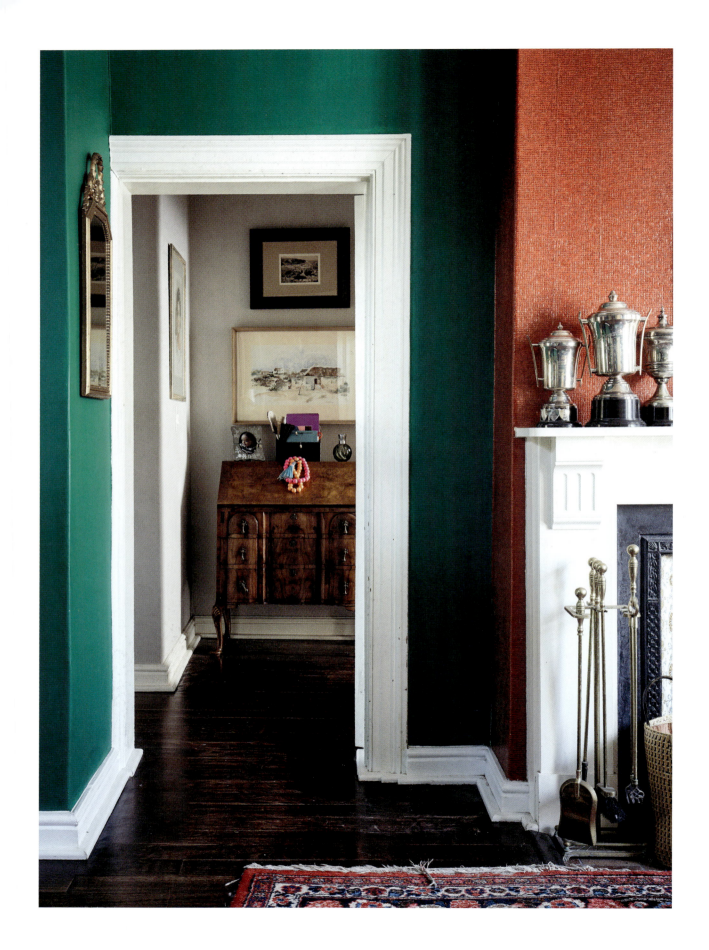

Sarah wasted no time painting the dining room, kitchen, and lounge walls in forest green, inspired by a ceramic beer mug she had discovered in an antique store (colour inspiration is everywhere!). The kitchen cupboards and doors transitioned from white to a bold, dashing blue – white, according to Sarah, is simply too 'blah.' An old grey oak cabinet was transformed with a delicious siren red. Beyond paint, Sarah finds inventive ways to incorporate colour and character. In the lounge, a woven-plastic floor mat was reimagined as upholstery for the coffee-table ottoman, demonstrating her knack for repurposing materials in unexpected ways. Her love of textures and objects extends to fabrics, lacquered boxes, ceramics, baskets, and antiques. Sarah's home is a tapestry of storied purchases and auction finds. Her art collection is just as eclectic: paintings inherited from her great-grandmother, framed tissue paper from an Italian pharmacy, a Picasso print… each piece contributes to the home's layered aesthetic, ensuring that every wall tells a story. A devoted admirer of the late British designer John Fowler – renowned for popularising English country-house style – she believes heritage and contemporary design can coexist beautifully when balanced thoughtfully.

Extending a single colour across multiple surfaces and rooms creates a seamless, enveloping effect that unifies your living spaces.

Ideal for those who find bold, high-energy palettes overwhelming, a muted colour approach allows you to incorporate a variety of shades subtly, enhancing your home's aesthetic without overpowering it. By opting for a subdued colour palette, your home can effortlessly adapt to your evolving tastes, providing endless possibilities for nuanced, layered designs in every room.

Choosing the right colour combinations for your space can be challenging, especially with so many tones and shades to consider. While natural light plays a crucial role, a great starting point is selecting a desaturated primary colour as your base. Sarah, for example, chose a muted forest green as her foundational hue. She then layered in neutral tones – off-white trimmings and dark brown flooring – to add depth. To enhance harmony, she incorporated natural elements like a wooden table, chairs, and curtains. These foundation colours create a subtle backdrop, allowing secondary and complementary colours (like the siren red cabinet and mantelpiece) to pop, resulting in a balanced and inviting atmosphere without the heaviness that darker tones can bring.

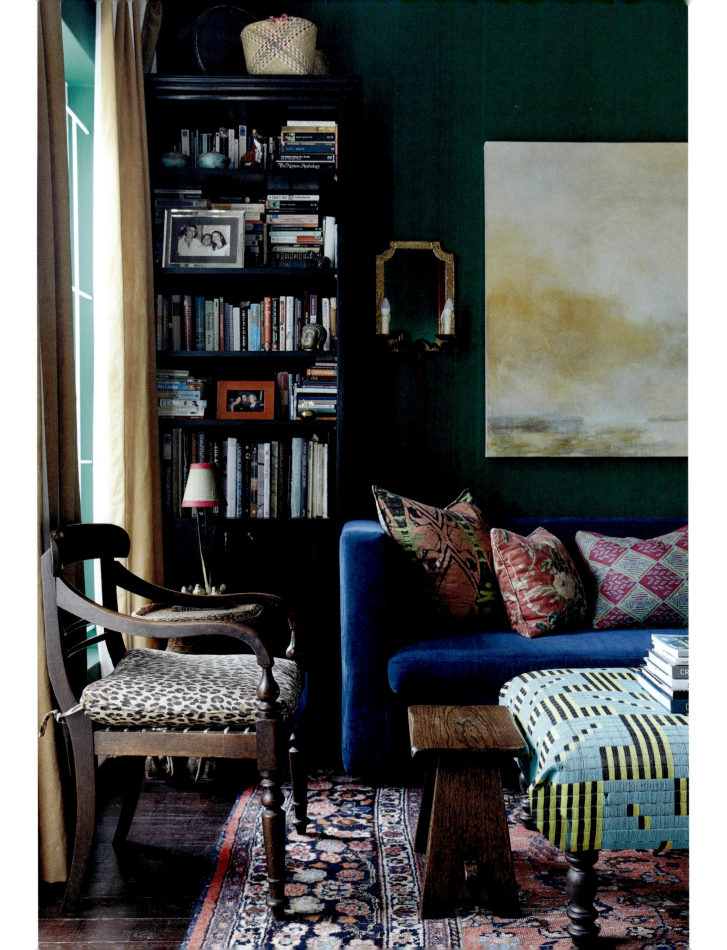

QUIRKY CURIOSITIES, MUTED COLOURS

COLOUR COMBINATIONS

COLOUR COMBINATIONS   DELIVERING THE UNEXPECTED

COLOUR SCHEME → SPLIT-COMPLEMENTARY

The Unexpected Red Theory – coined by Taylor Simon on TikTok – suggests that a room never truly looks complete until it includes a touch of red. Much like how a classic red lipstick can perfect an outfit, this design principle argues that adding even a small amount of red to a space where it wouldn't typically belong instantly makes the room feel more cohesive. In essence, a little (or a lot) of red can go a long way in making a space feel vibrant, unique, and full of life.

DELIVERING THE UNEXPECTED

Just off East London stands The Arc, a 22-storey tower rising from a red brick podium building that reflects the industrial heritage of its unique surroundings. European developer Ghelamco enlisted Sophie van Winden and Simone Gordon, founders of the interior design studio Owl and renowned for their unexpected and innovative approach, to dress up one of their show flats.

While the term show flat often raises images of neutral tones and conventional décor, Sophie and Simone set out to defy expectations. They crafted a bold and characterful aesthetic using sustainably and locally sourced fabrics, accessories, and furniture – incorporating repurposed materials wherever possible. In the living- and dining area of the two-bedroom apartment, a distinctive palette blends rich rust red – paying homage to the building's exposed brickwork – with muted greens and light blue. The use of bold colours and sculptural shapes feels fresh and light and never overpowering, creating an overall balancing act between serenity and boldness. Layered fabrics add depth and texture, preventing the space from feeling solely defined by blocks of colour. The master bedroom features a harmonious blend of pink and peach tones, accented by muted earthy greens, ochre yellow, and subtle metallics. A rich variety of textures, from silk grasscloth wallpaper to heavy bouclé and woven cotton

fabrics, enhances the room's tactile appeal. The soft green-hued walls serve as the perfect backdrop for the bold headboard, bold cushion fabrics, and playful lamps, adding depth and character to the space.

While red can be an energising and joyful addition to interiors, it is also a colour that attracts attention and has a longstanding association with danger (just about any traffic sign). But when applied thoughtfully, it softens these intense associations, transforming red elements into stylish and desirable focal points. Depending on how much red you're applying to a space, lean towards reds with brown or earthy undertones if you want to paint a whole room. It will give the space a more grounded, sophisticated feel. Opt for slightly lighter, brighter reds if you're after one or two accessories or an accent piece. The contrast that your preferred shade of red will create with the other colours within the room is another defining factor in the success of your scheme. In the show apartment's example, the red playfully contrasts with the blue and pastel tones, creating a dynamic balance while maintaining a shared sense of vibrancy. If you prefer a more understated elegance or are still getting comfortable with decorating with red, go for a mix of deep, dark reds accented with pops of bright red, all with warm undertones, as can be seen on pages 128-133..

DELIVERING THE UNEXPECTED

COLOUR COMBINATIONS

The unexpectedness of the chequered throw pillows is a bold, playful contrast to the warm, muted tones in the master bedroom.

Sophie and Simone went for a more contemporary feel by using a lacquered finish on the red sideboard. The gloss finish sits beautifully next to the soft blue of the wall.

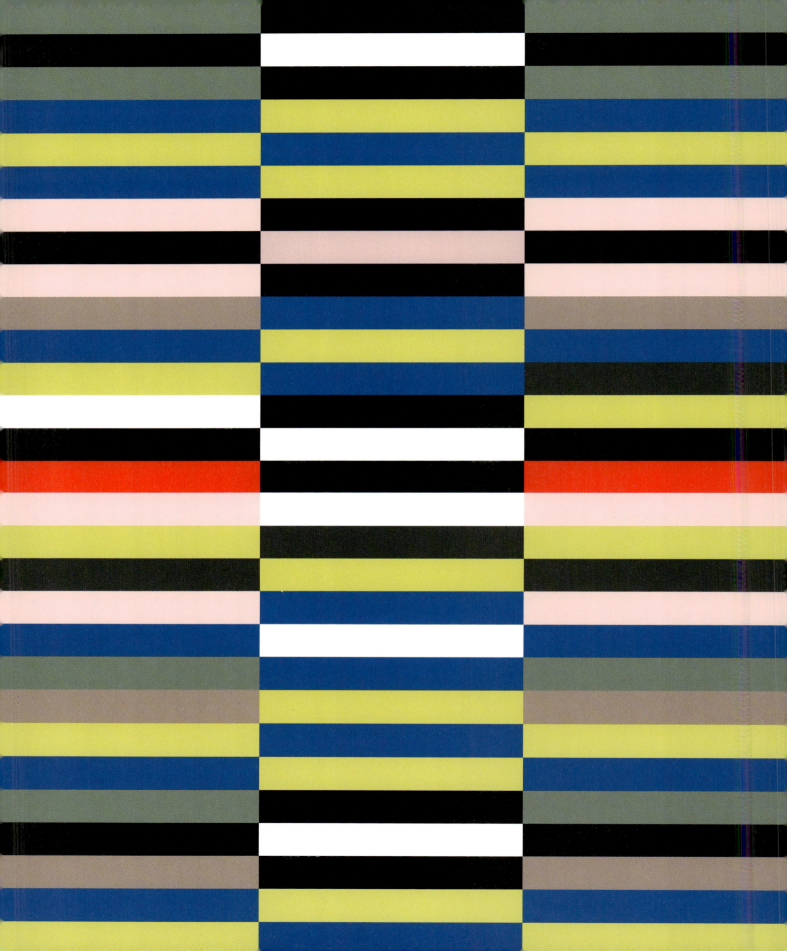

MADNESS TO THE METHOD COLOUR COMBINATIONS

COLOUR SCHEME → TETRADIC

Ultramarine is a pigment derived from the precious mineral lapis lazuli. It's the superlative blue, the end-all blue, but its production process makes it quite costly. Yves Klein Blue, created and patented by the artist Yves Klein, and Majorelle Blue, named after the famous garden in Marrakesh, Morocco, are both expensive variations. Fortunately, a more affordable synthetic alternative, cobalt blue, was developed in the 19th century, quickly becoming a staple in the modern design world.

MADNESS TO THE METHOD

When lyricist Paolo Antonacci first saw the 70-square-metre residence in a former warehouse, he immediately decided to buy it. Today it pulses with its own vibrant rhythm, a testament to the trust he placed in interior designer Stefania Passera to fully unleash her creative vision.

The warehouse, tucked away in the courtyard of an early 20th-century building, is a Lilliputian structure nestled among towering buildings along Milan's inner ring road, exuding a distinct post-industrial charm. The challenge of transforming the ground-floor space – with its barred windows and porcelain stoneware flooring – into a captivating, magical retreat which also reflected the resident's personality was entrusted to Stefania (whose own studio is featured on pages 136–141). Paolo had only two non-negotiables: the wallpaper in the bedroom, which he fell in love with at first sight, and blush pink as the dominant hue.

Stefania used the surreal, dreamlike atmosphere of the American-style wallpaper featuring stylised 1930s women lounging on the beach among palm trees, cacti, and parasols, set against a pink desert as a starting point. To counterbalance the delicacy of the pink and prevent it from feeling overly precious, she introduced two bold primary colours – cobalt blue and lemon yellow – which became the unifying elements of the design.

The entrance floor features 10x10 centimetre yellow tiles with blue grout, which extend up the steps and into a bathroom entirely in yellow. In the living room, the muted tones on the wooden cabinetry and walls help to ground the design, avoiding total chaos. Stefania has skilfully used colour to delineate the different areas of the shared space. The green carpet and sofa subtly define the living area, while the black-and-white striped rug in the dining area not only defines that space but also tempers what Stefania herself described as the 'madness'.

Cobalt blue is electrifying, which makes it the perfect colour to play with, even if neutrals are your thing. It instantly modernises a space and can be the ideal gateway to other colour combinations. By working in some strong contrasting colours, like yellow, orange, or pink, you get a pop art kind of feel. Geometric patterns, on the other hand, pair particularly well with it as they match the colours' energy, giving it that deliciously mad Memphis Milano feel.

You could also incorporate a piece of furniture in solid blue – whether it's an armchair, coffee table, or even a sofa. Keep the rest of the décor neutral to create a beautiful, sleek contrast. You can even experiment with accessories, from simple throw pillows to candle holders or even candles. The beauty of this approach is its flexibility – you can easily switch things up whenever you want, ensuring you don't tire of this daring hue too quickly.

The bedroom features a cool shade of pink, which is complemented by the blue ceiling and vibrant, rainbow-coloured 1970s armchairs.

COLOUR COMBINATIONS   ORANGE IS THE NEW BLACK

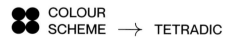

COLOUR SCHEME → **TETRADIC**

1970s design was a distinctive fusion of styles and influences, shaped by the cultural shifts and trends of the era. While bold geometric patterns and clashing colour palettes remain its most recognisable features, the decade's aesthetic was also playful, eclectic, and rich with nostalgia. Today's reinterpretation embraces its retro charm while offering a fresh, modern twist – infusing your home with the fun and funk of the 1970s without making it feel like a time capsule.

ORANGE IS THE NEW BLACK

COLOUR COMBINATIONS

ORANGE IS THE NEW BLACK

Located in a 1960s building in central Turin, interior designer Marisa Coppiano envisioned a carefully restored apartment – an interior that would reflect the era of the psychedelic 1960s and the freedom of expression of the 1970s.

The owner of the 100-square-metre house, a dear friend of interior designer Marisa Coppiano, entrusted himself completely to her vision for the interior. The selected finishes reinterpret materials and design solutions from both eras through a modern perspective. Curved lines characterise many of the furniture pieces, while a vibrant palette of tangerine, fuchsia, (electric) blue, and citrus lime captures the dynamic spirit of the time, creating a sense of excitement and youthful energy.

The 1970s have often been mocked for their more dubious design choices, such as plastic-covered furniture, orange-brown colour schemes, and thick shag carpets...just to name a few. But it was also a decade of cultural revolution, and this spirit of liberation and self-expression shone through in its bold and vibrant colour choices. Marisa's approach to the 1970s is refined and intentional, selectively embracing the best of 1970s style while leaving the outdated elements behind. She created, for example, two rounded breakthroughs in the wall in the living room – one a niche that can function as a wardrobe when needed and one that serves as a mirror. Along with increasing the perceived size and depth of a room, mirrors are a great way to brighten up a room. (But do keep in mind that your mirror should be hung near a source of light, like a window.) The relaxation area is centred around puffy, oversized sofas, chairs, and custom-made furniture pieces – classic designs from the era that still look as fresh and contemporary as the day they were created. The groovy curtains are another subtle nod to the 1970s. The warm wooden flooring flows throughout the apartment, establishing visual continuity.

Some people may find orange a difficult colour to work with in a design, but orange is a surprisingly versatile colour that will work alongside many other shades. It has less intensity than red and there are of course a multitude of different oranges out there. Bright shades are perfect if you are looking to bring joy and playfulness to a space. Alternatively, earthy and closer to terracotta shades are perfect for creating a more cosy feel (more about those on pages 66–71). Pairing perfectly with (dark) blues and greens, it's also the ideal solution for adding a pop of colour to otherwise muted spaces. In her design, Marisa combined a beautiful tangerine and vibrant fuchsia (not often thought of as an obvious colour combination, but how wrong this is!) with green and blue – opposite sides of the colour wheel. This clever mix gives the interior a contemporary, fresh vibe with strong contrasts, while maintaining balance and avoiding a visually overwhelming or overly 'groovy' feel.

ORANGE IS THE NEW BLACK

COLOUR COMBINATIONS

ORANGE IS THE NEW BLACK

COLOUR COMBINATIONS

The curved line defines the architecture of the spaces, with the green lacquered wall enclosing the house's laundry room.

Thank you

Thanks to my loves, Pim, Jet, and Cato.
Mum and Dad, Bas, Dieuwke, Steven, and
Willem. Greetje, Lodie, Marilou, Constantijn,
Jorieke, and Rob.
Thanks dear Anki, you know why.
Sabine and Marloes, for your support and
laughter (among other things). My life
would be so dull and grey without you all.
Sarah and Irene, thank you so much
for putting in the teamwork to make
the dream work.

Bibliography

Alexandra Loske, *Colour: A Visual History* (London: Octopus Publishing Group, 2019).

Kassia St. Clair, *The Secret Lives of Colour* (London: John Murray, 2016).

Photo credits

pp.10 – 19: Photos: Ramona Balaban / Living Inside, pp.20 – 29: Photos: Monica Spezia / Living Inside - Styling : Francesca Sironi, pp. 30 – 39: Photos: Valentina Sommariva / Living Inside Text: Alice Ida, pp. 40 – 47: Photos: Paolo Bramati / Living Inside – Styling: Daniela De Vito, pp. 48 – 55: Photos: Monica Spezia / Living Inside, pp. 56 – 63: Photos: Nathalie Krag / Living Inside – Styling: Giulia Deitinger– Interior Designer: Daniele Daminelli, pp. 64 – 71: Photos: Eve Campestrini / Living Inside, pp. 72 – 79: Photos: Richard Powers, pp. 80 – 89: Photos: Valentina Sommariva / Living Inside – Styling: Alice Ida, pp. 90 – 99: Photos: Richard Powers, pp. 100 – 109: Photos: Monica Spezia / Living Inside - Production : Alice Ida, pp. 110 – 117: Photos: Ramona Balaban / Living Inside, pp. 118 – 125: Photos: Monica Spezia / Living Inside - Production and styling: Sophie Wannenes, pp. 126 – 133: Photos: Monica Spezia / Living Inside, pp. 134 – 141: Photos: Fabrizio Cicconi / Living Inside - Styling: Francesca Davoli, pp. 142 – 151: Photos: Nathalie Krag / – Living Inside – Architect : Giuliano Andrea dell'UVA, pp. 152 – 161: Photos: Greg Cox / Bureaux / Living Inside – Production: Sven Alberding / Bureaux, pp. 162 – 171: Photos: Guillaume Grasset / Living Inside, pp. 172 – 181: Photos: John Ellis / Living Inside - Architects: Dufner Heighes, pp. 182 – 191: Photos: Andrè Nazareth / Living Inside - Styling: Simone Raitzik, pp. 192 – 201: Joanne Burgess – Photos: Rachael Smith / Living Inside, pp. 202 – 211: Photos: Monica Spezia / Living Inside – Production and styling : Francesca Sironi, pp. 212 - 219: Photos: Benedicte Drummond - Production: Laurence Dougier - Architect: Agence Marn - Interior design: Nicolas Payet, pp. 220 – 229: Photos: Warren Heath/ Bureaux/ Living Inside – Styling: Sven Alberding, pp. 230 – 237: Photos: Rachael Smith / Living Inside – Interior design: Sophie Van Winden - OWL DESIGN, pp. 238 – 245: Photos: Fabrizio Cicconi and Francesca Davoli / Living Inside, pp. 246 – 253: Photos: Barbara Corsico / Living Inside - Styling: Chiara dal Canto

Texts
Marlous Snijder

Copy-editing
Lisa Holden

Image Selection
Marlous Snijder
Irene Schampaert

Book Design
Irene Schampaert

If you have any questions or comments about the material in this book, please do not hesitate to contact our editorial team: art@lannoo.com

© Lannoo Publishers, Belgium, 2025
D/2025/45/119 – THEMA: AMR, WJK
Isbn 9789020954784

All rights reserved. No part of this publication may be reproduced or transmitted in any form or by any means, electronic or mechanical, including photocopy, recording or any other information storage and retrieval system, without prior permission in writing from the publisher. All rights are reserved, including those for text and data mining, AI training and similar technologies.

Every effort has been made to trace copyright holders. If, however, you feel that you have inadvertently been overlooked, please contact the publishers.